Gifts *from the* Pharaohs

CHRISTINE DESROCHES NOBLECOURT

Gifts *from the* Pharaohs

How Egyptian Civilization
Shaped the Modern World

Flammarion

Translated from the French by Jonathan Sly
Copyediting: Bernard Wooding
Design: Claude-Olivier Four
Proofreading: Chrisoula Petridis

Distributed in North America
by Rizzoli International Publications, Inc.

Originally published in French
as *Le Fabuleux Héritage de l'Égypte*
© Éditions SW Télémaque, 2004

English-language edition
© Flammarion, SA, 2007

www.editions.flammarion.com

07 08 09 10 4 3 2 1
ISBN-10: 2-0803-0562-X
ISBN-13: 978-2-0803-0562-6

Dépôt légal: 01/2007
Printed in Singapore by Tien Wah Press

The images in this book are from the private
collection of Christiane Desroches Noblecourt

Contents

Foreword   7

I   The Calendar   14

II   The Lion and the Locusts   36

III   The Frog: from Protohistory to the Christian Church   46

IV   Fish, Taboos, and Resurrection   58

V   The Game of Goose and the Greeks   70

VI   Saint George and Saint Christopher   82

VII   From Turquoise Mines to the Alphabet   100

VIII   Egyptian Medicine   116

IX   Architecture and its Heritage   128

X   Words that Traveled   152

XI   The Legacy of Egypt in Israel,
or Joseph and Egypt   164

XII   Wisdom   212

XIII   Theogamy, the Myth of the Mother Goddess,
and the Sacred Bark   226

XIV   The Secret of the Sanctuaries   254

Notes   286
Chronology   287
Further Reading   288

Foreword

My aim in this book is to introduce readers to the fundamental themes on which our own civilization is built, without resorting to tiresome academic explanations and bombastic prose. It will reveal ancient Egypt's pioneering role in terms in terms of the knowledge, wisdom, and humanity that it bequeathed to us. It remains a major inspiration for those wishing to discover their roots. Throughout my career as an Egyptologist, I have been struck, as have many of my colleagues, by the exceptional importance of animals in their symbolism, which has no equal elsewhere. Furthermore, in many instances, our civilization has adopted this animal imagery to express ideas not very far removed from their original meaning.

Scribes and illustrators used this symbolic bestiary to perpetuate the tradition of fables and legends and the distant Creator chose a considerable number of these creatures to enact his wide-ranging interventions.

Far from believing that certain human forms crowned with the heads of ibises, rams, cows, or even man himself were genuine images of divinities, each limited to a specific domain,

Artist's study (ostracon) illustrating a fable about a wolf and a goat. This Egyptian fable inspired Aesop, who in turn influenced La Fontaine. The wolf plays the oboe to hold the young goat captive.
Ramesside period,
Nineteenth dynasty

FACING PAGE:
Seth, the embodiment of confusion
Seth was one of five children engendered by the goddess Nut, the celestial vault. In his royal headdress, the *pschent*, he here represents a warrior. His animal head has still not been identified. To suggest his possibly Asian origins, he is wearing a loincloth originating from the continent.
Damascened bronze,
Early Saite Period,
Copenhagen Museum

The *Tilapia nilotica*, or Nile tilapia
This fish with pink fins, today known as a *bolti*, was called *inet* by the ancient Egyptians. It was once believed to convey the soul of the deceased in his passage to rebirth. Glazed terra cotta stone from Ramses II's palace to the east of the Nile Delta.
Egyptian Museum, Cairo

clerics knew these figures were one of the many expressions of divinity. When it came to depicting the afterlife to which Egypt aspired, the easiest way to translate something so unknown was to start with what people already knew—the visible and tangible—in order to express allusions and images. Sometimes we find a particular creature faithfully reproduced in the work of Aesop, or later in the work of the seventeenth-century French author La Fontaine, without losing anything of its deeper meaning. Take, for example, the star Sothis, or Sirius, which in ancient Egypt was represented by a dog from prehistory onwards; today, today it continues to lend its name to the Canis Major constellation of which it is part.

Another example: for thousands of years, funerary chambers were decorated with the ritualistic scene depicting the capture of the fish, *inet* (*Tilapia nilotica*), which enabled the dead to regain possession of their soul. In early Christianity, too, on cell walls in Egyptian monasteries, the soul of the dead was depicted by the fish, *ichthus*, the symbol of a victorious renascent Christ.

On occasion groups of animals were depicted together to illustrate a specific myth. Thus, by drawing a crouching baboon

in apparent conversation with a lioness, her prominent breasts dangling, the illustrator would have been referring to the key moment of the popular legend of the Distant Goddess. This legend starts with the Creator living happily in his palace with his beautiful, generous daughter, who fills all hearts with joy. The sprightly princess soon tires of this gilt-edged life and, one day, leaves the land for the south. The palace and the land are engulfed by despair. The powerful sovereign attempts to persuade his daughter to return, sending out messenger after messenger, but his daughter, hungry for freedom, refuses to come back even though Egypt is bereft of life and happiness. The king sends his final emissary, Thoth's monkey, a classic divine spirit, to use his renowned skills to woo the infidel back, recounting a thousand delightful fables as he leads her to the borders of Egypt, where she is soothed by the sound of the Nile's First Cataract. For ancient Egyptians, the image of the monkey in conversation with a lioness was enough to evoke the whole of this legend.

The very same story is also referred to in a more concise way in a single event: the Nile's inundation and the arrival of the Egyptian New Year. In the list of the months of the year,

Cats and mouse
Fragment of a satirical papyrus depicting a fable featuring cats serving a mouse-queen.
Ramesside period,
Nineteenth dynasty

The lion and the unicorn
The unicorn, of Syrian origin, was the symbol for a royal favorite in the New Kingdom. Here this "princess" is depicted playing *senet* with a lion, the symbol of the king. The two animals also appear on the English royal coat of arms.
Satirical papyrus,
Nineteenth dynasty

ABOVE, LEFT:
The zodiac sign of Cancer
This is based on the image of
the Egyptian scarab beetle.
This monumental sculpture
of the beetle on its high
pedestal can be seen in the
temple of Karnak to the
northwest of the sacred lake.
The sculpture was found
in the mortuary temple
of Amenophis III
on the west bank at Thebes.
New Kingdom,
Eighteenth dynasty

ABOVE, RIGHT:
Thoth's baboon tries to
persuade the lioness to return
home. Above, the nest of eggs
brooded by the vulture of the
south, where this scene takes
place, symbolizes the Distant
Goddess's pregnancy.
Ostracon (artist's study),
Nineteenth dynasty

the two adjacent signs at the center are Cancer (the scarab
beetle) and Leo (the lioness). The scarab is symbolic of the
moment the sun appears at dawn, in the "final hour of
night," when the scarab shunts his "ball" symbolizing the day
star. The scarab is followed by Leo, or the lioness, in the
calendar, who emerges with the incredible force and wealth
of the gushing waters of the new tide, with the same tide that
will fertilize Egypt for four months during the *peret* season,
bringing back joy and prosperity.

Naturally this wealth of animal symbols is far from being
our only heritage of the Pharaonic era. Ancient Egypt's
influence on us extends to many key areas of our civilization,
such as the solar calendar and the origins of the alphabet. Let
us not forget either their influence on the Hebrews, and on
common wisdom, medicine, architecture, customs, and
chemistry, as well as religion.

Egypt, more than its neighbors, endeavored to find
multiple forms of expression for these aspects, using different
images to express similar themes and notions. The Osiris
myth is one of the most famous applications of this. In it, the
kindly god is seen caught in a perpetual struggle against evil,

resulting in the death of the god and hope in the rebirth of
the martyr god.

However, the most important of the five divine principles
introduced into the world by Nut, the celestial vault, was the
first-born. Osiris became the protector and benefactor of the
country. His younger brother, Seth, represented disturbance,
a disturbance which was nevertheless necessary. He was
driven by his constant jealousy of his older brother, and he
twice tried to kill him. Finally, having cut him into sixteen
pieces (or fourteen according to a different legend), he threw
them into the Nile.

However, Isis, the god's sister-wife, was watching. She
transformed herself into a bird and fished her husband's remains
from the river and created the first mummy. Now, Osiris reigned
over the dead in the afterlife. He would judge them on entry and
became their master, protector, and model. Each year, mortals
knew of his presence through the flood. To live in his wake, the
dead also made their presence felt in the rising of the tide and
they too participated in the country's growth.

The religion of Osiris was born. Back on Earth, however,
Osiris's lineage had not been assured. Using her legendary

**Evocation of the myth
of the Distant Goddess**
The princess in the form
of a solar lioness, intoxicated
with freedom, beats her tail
to show her anger. We can see
from her pendulous breasts
that she has given birth to
cubs. The goddess Nekhbet
from the south, in the form
of a vulture, situates the
scene. Facing the lioness, the
baboon is trying to convince
her to return home. In the
fable the lioness represents
the Nile's flood and the
baboon is Thoth, god of
the calendar, who is trying
to avoid a delay in the
inundation.
Bas-relief from the Dakke
temple (Nubia), Late Period

**First representation
of the solar calendar.**
The twelve months of thirty
days are each depicted by
their first respective day of
twenty-four hours. The five
and a quarter days are placed
between the four-month block
on the left, and the other eight
months to the right. The
calendar should be read from
right to left and top to
bottom. First come the four
red months of the flood, then
space is left for the
epagomenal days (five and
a quarter). Next come the
"winter and spring" months
in green, and then the four
hot months in solar yellow.
To assist in understanding,
the later signs of the zodiac
have been juxtaposed beside
each month.
Tomb of Senenmut

FACING PAGE:
Osiris
The god Osiris, who reigns
over the world of the dead,
appears in all his majesty
beneath his royal canopy with
quadruple floral capitals. His
body swathed in a shroud, the
mummy stands ready for
resurrection, his face painted
green, the color of rebirth.
Theban tomb of Sennedjem,
Deir el-Medina,
Nineteenth dynasty

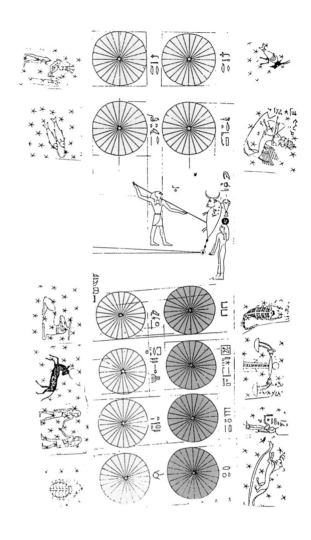

magic, Isis temporarily revived her husband's mummy and,
through this miracle, bore a son, Horus, to take up his father's
terrestrial throne.

This introductory overview of diverse themes from very
different areas of Egyptian civilization contains so many
coincidences that it is impossible to deny their shared origins. I
hope that these common aspects connecting the different
chapters will be accessible to the reader. They may even
surprise by their unexpected context, and will often resonate
most when they relate to ideas and rites that could have
inspired the art and thought of the Christian era.

I

The Calendar

The spirit of the flood
The spirit is crowned with
papyrus stems and is holding
two vases overflowing with
water, crouching in a cave
surrounded by the serpent of
the Earth. The illustration is
symbolic of the mythical
sources of the Nile and was the
source of the zodiac sign of
Aquarius.
Hadrian's Gate, Island of Philae,
Roman era

FACING PAGE:
Image of the Great Green
(*wadj wer*), the embodiment of
the flooding Nile. This rotund
spirit is covered in "threads of
water" suggestive of the Nile's
tide spreading throughout
Egypt over four months from
the end of July.
Temple of Sahure, Fifth dynasty

THE "FATHER OF GODS"

"The Nile, Egypt's sole river, was beneficially transformed
once a year by flooding. Due to its miraculous, providential
behavior, the river was worshipped as an inaccessible
divinity beyond the limits of the Universe." (E. Drioton)

At the end of the Pharaonic era, the sacred texts
of the temple of Edfu (third century BC), still continued
to praise the glory of the "Father of gods, the ancestor
that created the Ennead and who nourished the gods
by the sweat of his body. Men lived from his sweat until
another moment came, and the Eternal One, who never dies,
came in peace."

EGYPT BEFORE EGYPT

Let us try to imagine what life was like for those living way
back in the Paleolithic age, in what the anthropologist
Leakey has termed the "pebble culture," that is to say
a culture based on the uses of split flint.

On the terraces of the Theban mountain, flint tools
similar to "split flint" have been discovered by the

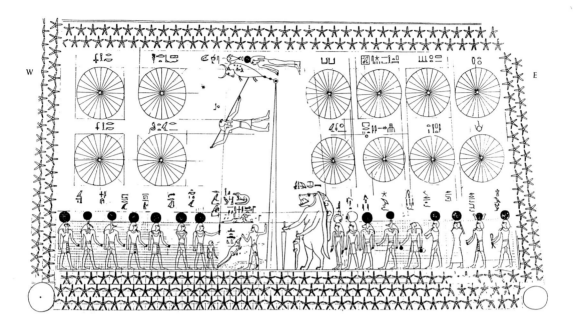

Senenmut's calendar featuring the three seasons
Representation of the first calendar. The twelve months are symbolized by twelve circles from top to bottom and left to right. There are the four months of the *akhet* season (flood), the first two months of the *peret* season (winter), the last two months of the *peret* season (spring), and four months of the *shemu* season (summer).
Senenmut's burial chamber, Deir el-Bahri, Eighteenth dynasty

prehistorian Debono, the prehistorian and anthropologist Professor Biberson, and the geomorphologist Professor Coque. These tools are now conserved in the Department of Egyptian Antiquities at the Louvre in Paris. They were no doubt dropped by distant primitive ancestors of the fellahin, living a predatory existence on the high plateaus, according to the vegetation available. It is possible that elephants and giraffes also lived on these plateaux, as suggested in the primitive drawings on the sides of the famous Theban peak, which is a natural pyramid.

From their lofty position, these nomads would have noticed the huge expanse of water of the gigantic river estuary much further to the north, an area that later became the Nile Delta. To the south, their meanderings may have led them to the place where, later, the calmer waters of the Nile, the White Nile, were joined by those of the Blue Nile from Lake Tana in Ethiopia. This huge gulf would swell yearly, bringing with it alluvia torn from the lands through which it flowed.

Animal symbols
The image of a giraffe,
graffiti at the foot of the
natural pyramid.
The image of an elephant
engraved at the foot of
"The Lady of the Peak."
Western Thebes

Late prehistoric graffiti
At the foot of the natural
pyramid of rocks on the west
bank at Thebes, early man
engraved the outlines of
animals he encountered.
The giraffe is instantly
recognizable.
Prehistoric drawings, Western
Thebes

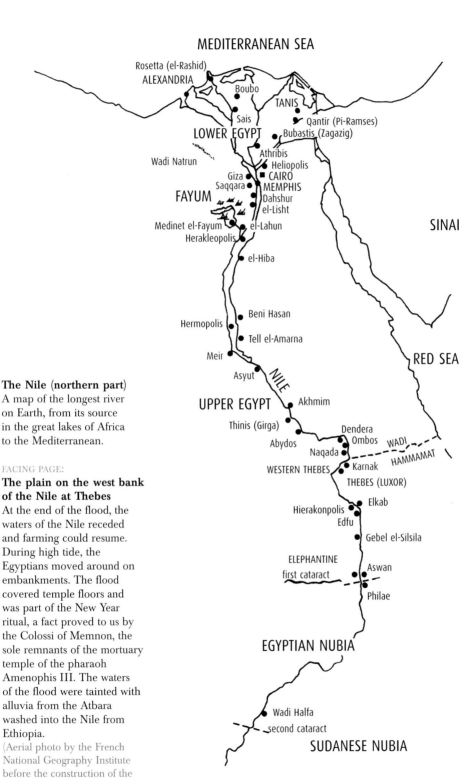

The Nile (northern part)
A map of the longest river
on Earth, from its source
in the great lakes of Africa
to the Mediterranean.

FACING PAGE:

**The plain on the west bank
of the Nile at Thebes**
At the end of the flood, the
waters of the Nile receded
and farming could resume.
During high tide, the
Egyptians moved around on
embankments. The flood
covered temple floors and
was part of the New Year
ritual, a fact proved to us by
the Colossi of Memnon, the
sole remnants of the mortuary
temple of the pharaoh
Amenophis III. The waters
of the flood were tainted with
alluvia from the Atbara
washed into the Nile from
Ethiopia.
(Aerial photo by the French
National Geography Institute
before the construction of the
Aswan High Dam)

MEDITERRANEAN SEA

Rosetta (el-Rashid)
ALEXANDRIA
Boubo
TANIS
Sais
Qantir (Pi-Ramses)
LOWER EGYPT
Bubastis (Zagazig)
Athribis
Wadi Natrun
Heliopolis
Giza
CAIRO
Saqqara
MEMPHIS
FAYUM
Dahshur
el-Lisht
Medinet el-Fayum
el-Lahun
SINAI
Herakleopolis

el-Hiba

Beni Hasan
Hermopolis
Tell el-Amarna
Meir
RED SEA
Asyut
NILE

UPPER EGYPT
Akhmim

Thinis (Girga)
Dendera
Abydos
Ombos
WADI
Naqada
Karnak
HAMMAMAT
WESTERN THEBES
THEBES (LUXOR)
Elkab
Hierakonpolis
Edfu
Gebel el-Silsila
ELEPHANTINE
Aswan
first cataract
Philae

EGYPTIAN NUBIA

Wadi Halfa
second cataract
SUDANESE NUBIA

The Theban mountain
In late prehistoric times, the fringes of the Saharan piedmont in Thebes were covered in water. Only the natural pyramid, the "Lady of the Peak," was exposed.
Western Thebes (west bank)

THE APPEARANCE OF THE NILE

When, in the course of several million years, the water level of this enormous lake fell, the alluvial layers born by the water had built up considerably. They eventually formed the valley of the Nile in the Upper Paleolithic era. During the Neolithic period, populations then settled by the water, as the land was so fertile that all kinds of seed could grow and flourish even before the sun had risen and disappeared beyond the horizon one hundred and twenty times.

THE LUNAR CALENDAR

Another way of measuring time was to use the moon's mysterious phases, the intervals of which were carefully studied by the early Egyptians. The lunar cycle naturally presented a number of visual advantages, which ensured its long use.

THE NEOLITHIC AGE

The first Neolithic shelters were made out of branches. Later, man learned how to fashion from the Nile's mud. These huts

Theban plain
The high water from late prehistoric times retreated, permitting agriculture.

in turn were replaced by rectangular dwellings made out of what was essentially the precursor of bricks, made from humus left by the river mixed with burned straw. The building materials people needed were deposited by the Nile, and people continued to use them to build houses until the modern age.

The composition of burial sites discovered in Neolithic dwelling areas proves that the occupants of these fertile banks already based their sense of survival on rituals. Their early funerary materials, including small earthenware pottery figurines of humans and animals, reveal their belief in the magic nature of the Nile's deposits. This was also symbolized by the placing of seeds in cups and bowls and in the decoration of vases, cups, and chests with scenes painted with ocher.

THE MARK OF ETHIOPIA

One of the most common motifs of these scenes is that of a plant, now identified as the Ethiopian wild banana tree (*Musa ensete*). Often too, there is the image of a boat with multiple oars, a possible reference to a journey or arrival by river. To me, in view

Neolithic vase
Vessel decorated with
a picture of a boat
with many oars.
Painted pottery,
Gerzean Period

of what later texts tell us, these vessels may evoke the annual flood, during which the dead were said to undergo transformation. The illustration of the *Musa enseta* therefore refers to the source of the annual tide, which brought alluvium torn from the banks of Ethiopia's Atbara River, along with wild banana trees.

For the prehistoric Egyptian, unaware of the White Nile's source, Ethiopia must have appeared as the source of the inundation, a land which would later be known as the "land of the god." The Nile, therefore, was crucial to the religious thinking of this early people, who already seemed to believe in some future destiny and the forces governing it.

THE ROLE OF THE DOG STAR

As the Egyptians adopted a sedentary lifestyle as farmers, they quickly became aware of the time lapses between the moment the flood arrived, the time it took to spread over arable land, its disappearance, and its return when the parched soil most needed it. The Nile dwellers' remarkable faculties of observation meant they noticed phenomena regularly preceding the periodic rise in the tide. They were experienced stargazers and eagerly studied the constellations, the most important of which, in their eyes (apart from the Great and Little Bear) were those that resembled a dog. The brightest of such stars was called *sepedet*, or Sothis to the Greeks, Sirius to us. This magnificent star was invisible seventy days a year, then made its return at dawn as the sun was rising. This phenomenon, it was noticed, preceded the inundation and gave rise to the ancient Egyptian New Year, marking the start of the period between the Nile's tides.

THE BIRTH OF THE SOLAR CALENDAR

The solar calendar was logically divided into three periods, dictated above all by agricultural activity. The first period was composed of one hundred and twenty sunrises and sunsets, when the farmer prepared his land, and planted and harvested the majority of his crops. This period, including the last two months of winter and the first two of spring, was called *peret* (the sewing of the seed, germination, and growing).

The following season, *shemu*, was the same length of four months, and was the season when the final harvests were

Sothis in the form of a dog
Statuette of a small dog symbolizing Sothis (Sirius), the brightest star of the Canis Major constellation.
Carved chlorite, Late Period, Musée du Louvre, Paris

The Great Dog

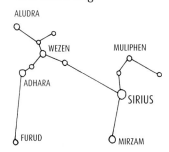

The Canis Major constellation as seen in the night sky.

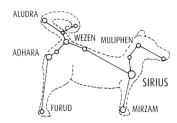

The same constellation with dotted lines to highlight the canine shape of the stars.
Drawing by C. Desroches Noblecourt

reaped, such as flax and grapes. During this period, the ground would start to warm as the level of the river dropped. Irrigation channels would dry out and the increasing heat made work difficult, leading to a decrease in production. The name *shemu* is the word from which the Arabic word "hammam" derives, in other words, "summer."

The inundation finally came at the start of the last four-month period, signaled by the arrival of the Sothis star. This was said to be a period of plenitude, *akhet*, during which the arable land was covered and fertilized by water once more.

The first day of the flood, New Year's Day, was celebrated by the ceremony of *wepet senet*, or "the opening of the year." Early inscriptions tell us that, before the end of the Predynastic period, inhabitants of this blessed land had long held notions of this cycle, and attributed a precise meaning to the word *renpet*, or year. The first day of the year was dedicated to science, knowledge, and intelligence or, as they saw it, to the divinity by the name of Thoth, incarnated in particular by the baboon that naturally originated in the kingdom of Punt, in Ethiopia, the "land of the god."

The ideal flood
The perfect Nile flood reached a height of sixteen cubits (twenty-seven feet). The phenomenon was so renowned that the Romans created a statue of the flooding Nile, represented by a powerful man surrounded by sixteen children. The figure symbolized the perfect flood, the embodiment of *hilaritas*, joy itself.

EPAGOMENES

In the solar calendar, commanded by the Nile and its tides, each of the three seasons comprised one hundred and twenty sunrises and sunsets. According to the rise and fall of the temperature, astronomers divided each season into four sets of thirty complete "revolutions" of the sun, each corresponding to a month of thirty days. Each month was divided into three "weeks," or *decans*, each of ten days. The ancient Egyptian year was thus composed of three hundred and sixty days, meaning there were five and a quarter days missing from the period separating each flood. These days were regarded as additional days, and the Egyptians called them "the days upon the year." Later, the Greeks referred to this short period as *epagomenes*.

A quarter day was still missing and priests eager to respect nature's own rhythms had to account for it. This fraction, they claimed, was left for the intervention of god. Farmers were the first to respect it, because their crops were bound by the regular rhythm of the seasons. However—and here I must simplify and disregard the difficulties and contradictions encountered—administrations generally seem to have neglected this quarter day on a systematic basis, which meant a day was

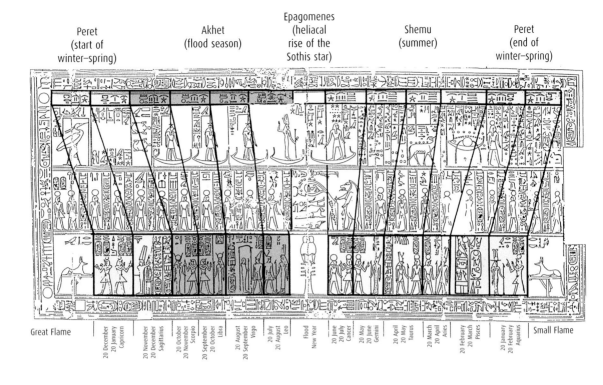

Peret (start of winter–spring) · Akhet (flood season) · Epagomenes (heliacal rise of the Sothis star) · Shemu (summer) · Peret (end of winter–spring)

Great Flame | 20 December 20 January Capricorn | 20 November 20 December Sagittarius | 20 October 20 November Scorpio | 20 September 20 October Libra | 20 August 20 September Virgo | 20 July 20 August Leo | Flood New Year | 20 June 20 July Cancer | 20 May 20 June Gemini | 20 April 20 May Taurus | 20 March 20 April Aries | 20 February 20 March Pisces | 20 January 20 February Aquarius | Small Flame

lost with every four floods; two at the end of eight. For *annus vagus*, or "wandering" calendar, and the official calendar to coincide, Egyptians had to wait 4 x 365 years, or 1,460 years, a period known as the Sothic cycle to Egyptians.

The omission of this quarter day in administrative time management was very inconvenient for scribes, and we know that sometimes they complained that real seasons did not match administrative ones, which obviously no longer applied due to discrepancies in the calendar; sometimes the harvest festival would be celebrated administratively in the middle of winter.

Priests and farmers, however, remained as faithful as possible to the real cycles of months and seasons, sometimes making adjustments for the slightest delay in the arrival of their providential tide, dependent as it was on rainfall and the melting of snow near the great African lakes.

LEGENDS

Many religious legends were associated with the days and months of the year. One of the most striking provides the explanation for the presence of the extra days, one that much

Ceiling of the Ramesseum
The horizontal line of the calendar carved into the ceiling of the Ramesseum coincides exactly with the order of the signs of the zodiac. The start of the calendar corresponds to the last two months of winter (Aquarius and Pisces). The end of the calendar corresponds to the two first months of winter (Sagittarius and Capricorn).
Temple of Ramses II, Nineteenth dynasty, Western Thebes

later would have a considerable effect, a subject that is revisited
in the Old Testament on the subject of Adam and Eve.

According to Egyptian mythology, the Creator created
the solar forces, Shu and Tefnut, and then created Geb and
Nut: the Earth and Sky. Geb and Nut lived closely entwined
as husband and wife; however, divine instruction forbade
them from ever having intercourse. Nut and Geb
transgressed the word of the Creator and terrible punishment
ensued. Shu wrenched the Sky from the Earth, and raised the
body of Nut to form the celestial vault. Meanwhile, Geb
struggled to join his true love but was held on the ground by
Shu; his efforts to join her gave birth to the mountains. Nut
was pregnant though, and divine forms intervened to allow
Nut to give birth to quintuplets. Osiris, Isis, Nephthys, Seth,
and Horus were born to watch over humanity, and the
charitable Creator added five extra days to the year.

THE MEASURE OF TIME

Astronomer-priests attempted to address the problem of the
length of hours in the calendar. For the Egyptians, the day

started at sunrise and the night at sundown. Whatever the
season, they divided light or dark periods into twelve sections.
Proof of this is provided by clepsydras, early water clocks. The
clepsydra was a truncated recipient filled with water that
dripped through a small opening in the bottom. Inside the
container, on its circular sides, was marked the time lapse
between hours, according to the seasons, which made the gaps
between hour marks different. Clepsydras were adapted by the
Greeks, and particularly the Romans, who used them to
measure time.

CALENDARS

Like the majority of ancient civilizations, Egypt had lunar
calendars, some of which may be compared to those
used in Muslim countries today. Under pressure from
scribes, and no doubt with royal support, the civil,
"wandering" calendar and the official solar calendar were
adjusted by the first Pharaohs of the Ptolemaic period.
These reforms were never carried through, no doubt for
religious reasons still unclear to us.

**Origin of the myth
of Adam and Eve**
Because they disobeyed the
creator, Geb and Nut were
separated for eternity. Nut
became the celestial vault and
Geb turned into the Earth. In
his struggle to join his loved
one, Geb formed the
mountains.
Funerary papyrus,
Egyptian Museum, Cairo

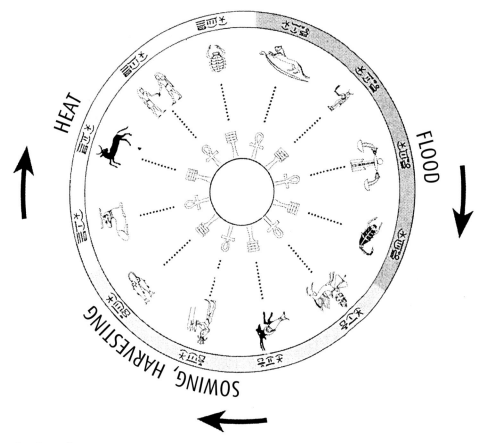

HEAT

FLOOD

SOWING, HARVESTING

Inside of a clepsydra

As an aid, the signs of the zodiac have been depicted around the perimeter.

Drawing of a clepsydra,
Eighteenth dynasty,
Egyptian Museum, Cairo

A clepsydra

The outside of a clepsydra in the form of a truncated cone. The recipient was filled with water, which dripped through a small hole in the base. A series of lines marked on the inside made it possible to tell the time by reading the water level. This water clock was invented by an Egyptian physician in the eighteenth dynasty.

Drawing of a clepsydra,
Eighteenth dynasty,
Egyptian Museum, Cairo

NEW YEAR

Whether the calendar was based on the phases of the sun or moon, the New Year was celebrated by all Egyptians. New Year came when the flood, or *hapy*, returned to feed the arable land. It was a festival celebrated particularly in the countryside and temples. On this special day, in their terrace-covered temples, priests appeared amid great ceremony, bearing the statue of their religion in its *naos*, so that the first rays of the dawn sun heralding the new era would shine through the open temple doors and offer their blessing. From the terrace tops, the New Year was proclaimed from temple to temple. The dykes at the entrance to irrigation canals were destroyed and the fresh fertilizing water spread over the parched fields and families celebrated with music in boats bedecked with flowers, followed by banquets with singing and dancing.

In Thebes, the huge vase of the god Amun, the "Hidden," was ceremoniously carried aloft on wooden poles. The vase was fitted with a cover representing the divine ram, and filled with the new water drawn by officiating priests from the river's edge or from temple canals. In archeological excavations of Karnak's great sanctuary, researchers have unearthed the sloping gallery that priests used to access the grand canal to greet the sacred water.

***Hapy*, the spirit of the flood**
Hapy, usually represented as a pot-bellied man with pendulous breasts, is portrayed here emerging from the water, crowned with three papyrii. He presents a tray of gifts filled with food.
Bronze statuette,
Saite Period,
Musée du Louvre, Paris

Celebration of New Year
Sovereigns and priests proceeding to the terrace of the temple to celebrate the New Year. The *naos* containing the divine statue is being carried up the staircase inside the pylon.
Temple of Dendara,
Late Period (Greco-Roman)

A concert
Musicians in concert during an important festival. The harp is typically Egyptian, but the lyre is of Semitic origin.
Tomb painting,
Eighteenth dynasty,
Western Thebes

Birth of the Sun
A representation of the dog Sothis contemplating the solar child, Harpocrates, to whom she has just given birth.
Glazed terra cotta,
Middle Kingdom,
Egyptian Museum, Cairo

In the city, delegations of senior civil servants headed toward the palace of the Pharaoh, the *per-aar* ("great house"). They made their way to the mortuary temple of the ruling king, led by ambassadors from allied countries offering exquisite gifts to the king and queen. Relatives and friends also exchanged gifts.

Small vases full of the miracle water circulated around Egypt and people wished each other a fine "opening to a beautiful year" (*wepet renpet neferet*). To foreign sovereigns, the Pharaoh would even send jars of sacred water, which were said to ensure fecundity. And people came from abroad to Egypt to draw water from the flood.

FROM SACRED WATER TO THE DOG DAYS

Among the most frequent gifts was the image of the dog, or *canicula* as Romans called it when they arrived in Egypt. From the Middle Kingdom onward, the dog of Sothis started appearing as an earthenware figurine on a plinth facing a naked boy. The boy in question was Horus, the sun child, and symbol of the rising sun. Well into the Ramesside era,

the Sothis star was represented on calendars by the image of an elegant young woman floating through the sky on a boat, not far from Orion.

During the Roman period, the bases of cups used for drinking the sacred water were decorated with the relief image of the *canicula*, straddled by a charming feminine Sothis riding sidesaddle. In Egypt, New Year coincided with the hottest times of the year. In the sky, the twinkling dog star lent its name to this canicular time of year: dog days.

Lady at a banquet
A lady taking part in a banquet. The charming young servant girls not only served food to guests, they also doused them with perfume and dressed them in garlands of flowers.
Tomb painting,
Eighteenth dynasty,
Western Thebes

Procession of the vase of Amun
The great vase of Amun with a lid in the shape of a ram's head. The vase was filled with new water from the flood and carried by priests in a procession from the temple of Amun to Karnak.
Tomb of Panehesy,
Eighteenth dynasty,
Western Thebes

Small "New Year's jar"
During the Saite Period, vases
like this one were filled with
holy water from the new
flood and exchanged as gifts.
The neck was often decorated
with a pair of baboons,
who came from the source
of the Nile. On one side
of the belly, the cow Hathor
appears on a bark against
a background of papyrii.
On the other side, the central
subject symbolizes the top
of Hathor's golden sistrum.
Glazed terra cotta, Saite Period,
Egyptian Museum, Cairo

Orion and Sothis
Ceiling decoration in the
burial chamber of Senenmut.
In the sky, Orion is preceded
by the Sothis star, which
appears as an elegant maiden.
Tomb of Senenmut,
Eighteenth dynasty,
Deir el-Bahri (Western Thebes)

THE INTERVENTION OF JULIUS CAESAR

When Julius Caesar visited Egypt, Cleopatra managed
to retain him for a while. While there in 45 BC, one of his
first concerns was to assign the Alexandrine scholar Sosigenes
to the task of switching the Roman lunar calendar to that
of the Egyptian temples, who regularly updated the days
of the year. He himself declared it was the "only intelligent
calendar to have ever existed in human history" and
adopted it in Rome with one small correction prepared by
Ptolemy II Euergetes. The calendar then went on to enjoy
similar fortune the whole world over. Gaul too had its own
version, with twelve months mainly associated with agrarian
names based on the solar instances of light and Osirian
instances of darkness, in other words, on the eternal cycle of
life, death, and resurrection. The Egyptian zodiac, in its general
form as we know it today, appeared in the Late Period.
Its twelve signs illustrate essential aspects of activities or
legends attributed to each month of the Egyptian solar
calendar, as we shall see later on.

This calendar and its New Year, introduced into Europe
by Julius Caesar, were soon adopted by ecclesiastical Christian
authorities in the early Middle Ages, without apparent changes. In
keeping with the wishes of several popes, however, in particular
Gregory XIII, who reformed parts of it in 1582, the dog day
period beginning the year was abandoned. The New Year was
moved to autumn, before finally being fixed at the end of
December. The new calendar now incorporated some pagan
festivals among its Christian celebrations.

EXCURSUS

After the French Revolution, the new revolutionary government
called upon Fabre d'Églantine to attribute new names to the
calendar so as to better illustrate the stages of the year.
D'Églantine's version featured the months ventôse, pluviôse, and
fructidor, whose names evoked the climate and the growing
cycle, and referred directly to the Egyptian zodiac calendar, the
source of which came from Latin textbooks. Evidence of this can
be seen by his recycling of Egyptian festivals such as the five
"epagomenal days" that he incorporated into his calendar. In
response to the new age, he called them the "sansculottidés,"
after the revolutionary sansculottes.

Image of eternity
The goddesses of the bark of
the day (left) and the bark of
the night (right), who
eternally pass the solar sphere
between them.
Funerary casket of Taho,
Saite Period, Musée du Louvre.

Fragment of a drinking vessel
Recipient used for drinking
sacred water at New Year.
The scene shows the Sothis
she-dog being ridden
sidesaddle by the Sothis
human image of the goddess.
The background represents
Osiris's vine, which would
have been ripe for harvest at
the moment of the tide's
arrival at the end of July.
Graywacke, Greco-Roman
Period, Musée du Louvre, Paris

II

The Lion
and the Locusts

The Lion

Honor comes where honor is due. Let us consider the case of the lion, which is deservedly known as the "king of the animals."

While early prehistoric Egyptians did not fear encountering lions in their everyday surroundings, they were sufficiently informed of their existence to draw illustrations on slates of the beast conquering their human enemies and preparing to devour them, or as a victor in depictions of an enemy citadel.

The lion's awesome nature and impressive bearing make it a symbol of mastery, the incarnation of incontestable chiefdom which, when tamed, can be used in the service of prestige and power, a wild feline whose power is channeled for good purpose. Of all members of the Egyptian bestiary, it is the animal that has been most studied, and while some aspects remain unclear, it is certain that the valiant lion was identified with the Egyptian sovereign.

The animal lends its body to that of the sphinx (*pa shesep ankh* in Egyptian), which is often portrayed with a human head, or that of a hawk or ram, depending on the divine form to which it is associated. The profiles of two lions sitting back to

ABOVE, LEFT:
Ramses II
The Pharaoh parading as victor on his chariot accompanied by his lion.
Aron Simbal,
Nineteenth dynasty

ABOVE, RIGHT:
The Royal Hunt of Tutankhamun
This dagger sheath belonging to the young king features a hunt for the wild bull and ibex, a scene enlivened by the zeal of the royal lion and cheetah.
Gold, Eighteenth dynasty,
Egyptian Museum, Cairo

FACING PAGE:
The sarcofagus of Khonsu
(see page 40)
Nineteenth dynasty,
New Kingdom,
Egyptian Museum, Cairo

Sarcophagus of Khonsu
In the upper panel, the sun
is seen rising between the
mountains on the horizon
flanked by two lions,
back to back.

FACING PAGE:
Throne of Tutankhamun
When the king was sitting on
his ceremonial throne, he was
identified with the sun rising
between two mountains on
the horizon, symbolized by
the lion's heads.
Wood, gold, and colored
molten glass,
Eighteenth dynasty,
Egyptian Museum, Cairo

back parallel the mountains in the background, symbolizing
yesterday and tomorrow, between which the day's sun shines.

Lions' mouths were used in early ancient Egypt to decorate
funerary furniture on which the dead would sit in the afterlife.
The deceased's throne was framed by two lions' heads, the
presence of which were thought to make the deceased shine
like the sun. The most stunning example of this use of lions'
heads is on Tutankhamun's magnificent "throne" (Cairo
Museum). Much earlier in the Old Kingdom, the powerful
Khafra was represented as a statue on a seat that was less
ornamental than that of Tutankhamun, but which was
nevertheless decorated and protected by two lion's heads.

The custom was perpetuated by the Romans and medieval
sovereigns, who liked to appear, in certain illuminations, sitting
on a kind of folding stool, defended by lions' heads. The
Romans, meanwhile, first encountered the lion in Egypt,
guarding temples and palaces. So, they adopted the lion's head
as guardian of their own doorframes, and it later appeared as
gargoyles, latches, and temple locks. In Roman fountains, water
leapt from lions' mouths, and any manner of creature was
slipped between the lion's open jaws.

However, before the lion was tamed by and for the king, it
also represented extreme violence, a danger requiring
extinction. Hunts were specially organized to this end, and
famous texts and reliefs testify to the royal lion hunts. One
unique historical example is supplied by a very rare object
contained in the funerary treasures of Queen Ahhotep.

THE DAGGER OF QUEEN AHHOTEP

Ahhotep, one of the most valiant royal women of the early part
of the New Kingdom, supported her husband and sons' war
efforts to beat back Egypt's invaders, the Hyksos. Apparently as
acknowledgment of this, the liberator of Egypt, Ahmose, laid a
military decoration in his mother's tomb, three golden "flies of
valor," an Egyptian military award, and a dagger illustrated

with a curious combat scene. On the right is a lion bounding in pursuit of a galloping bull fleeing crazily in the direction of four enormous locusts displaying Olympian calm.

The Locusts

At first sight, the composition is straightforward: the wild bull is mercilessly chased down by the lion or king, but its flight is derisively halted by four fantastical plump, placid, yet resolute locusts. The scene may seem humorous, but when placed in the context of the age and Egypt's troubles at the time, this dagger, a gift for the beloved queen mother, is certainly no joke. The significance of the locust in Egypt needs explaining to grasp the symbolism of the scene.

Firstly, contrary to popular opinion, the locust in ancient Egypt was never considered a pest, whether free-flying or in symbolic representations. Where texts are disparaging, the locust is depicted as dangerous and as capable of ravaging harvests. Their role as one of "Egypt's scourges" is more a product of the Bible's writers later on. While the disastrous effects of crickets in Africa and Mesopotamia, both in antiquity and today, are well documented, in ancient Egyptian writings no allusion is made to the kind of devastation recorded in Eastern, Palestinian, or Assyrian texts.

Gargoyle, temple at Edfu

Dagger decoration
This dagger is conserved in the Musée du Louvre, Paris. Its animal frieze is slightly less elegant than that of "The Royal Hunt of Tutankhamun" dagger conserved in the Egyptian Museum, Cairo (page 39).
Bronze,
Eighteenth dynasty,
Musée du Louvre, Paris

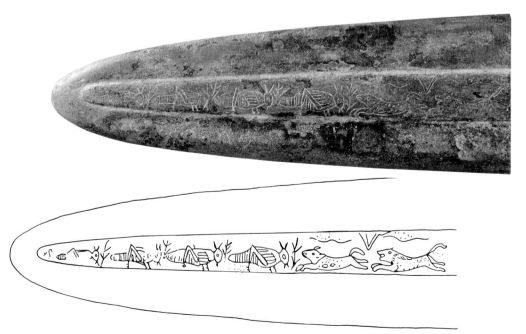

Locust in the swamps
The locust represented the battle for good. In this decoration for a funerary chapel, it has a protective symbolism. The evil hippopotamus is placed at the bottom of the water.
Painted relief in a tomb, Saqqara, Fifth dynasty

The dagger of Iahhotep
The Queen Mother Iahhotep was a valiant wartime companion to her husband and two sons. As a tribute for her actions, she received this gold dagger. Copies of the dagger, in less noble metals, were offered to the brave in battle.
Gold,
Early eighteenth dynasty,
Egyptian Museum, Cairo

The locust, instead, generally suggested the idea of multitude, comparable to groups of soldiers "swarming like locusts," ready to decimate the enemy. The locust is often represented with the souls of the dead, sitting near the scales that weigh up their life's deeds. It is also used to depict the king taking flight in the sky. Objects decorated with the locust's image are also important here: cosmetic jars, combs, and amulets to defend against attacks and for the preservation of ointments. In the Nilotic landscape, the locust had an important decorative and protective role, which included the illustrated ceilings of funerary chapels.

The locusts on Queen Ahhotep's dagger, then, can be interpreted as signifying the sovereign's very own formidable protective force, the army. The scene on the dagger doubtless conjures up the prince's fierce efforts to rid the country of its Asian invaders. So determined was he that he took the battle beyond Egyptian territory, taking Sharuhen, a Hyksos stronghold, near Gaza in southern Palestine, after a siege that lasted three years. In the light of this, the figurative scene depicted on the dagger takes on a very real dimension.

THE MEANING OF THE DAGGER'S SCENE

The lion chasing the wild bull is obviously the king pushing the enemy out of the country. The army is ritually figured by four locusts, no doubt to symbolize their influence at all four corners of the country. The figure of the locust was used to rebut and reduce evil, and it was also depicted on amulets and in the bucolic decors of funerary chapels as a symbol of protection.

The Legacy

Again we see how Egyptian symbolism, this time that of the locust, was passed on to the western world and medieval iconography. Locusts are to be found in the *moralia* of Pope Gregory the Great as the symbol of the *conversa gentilitas*, the pagans who rallied round Christ, forming into swarms of locusts to battle against Satan. Furthermore, a thirteenth-century capital in the basilica at Vézelay in central France features a locust bearing down on a basilisk, the figure of the Antichrist. In the fourteenth century, a painting attributed to Giovanni Baronzio from Rimini depicts the Madonna with the baby Jesus, who is holding a huge locust in his left hand.

Thus, one day, the symbol of the locust, a valiant soldier in the defense against aggression, took flight from the banks of the Nile to enlighten Western Christians with its message of providence.

Locust recipient
The image of the locust brought good fortune and decorated all kinds of toiletry items, especially ointment jars. The symbol protected the quality of the product it contained and the person who used it.
Schist,
Sixth dynasty,
Metropolitan Museum of Art,
New York

Capital, from the basilica of La Madeleine
Vézelay, central France

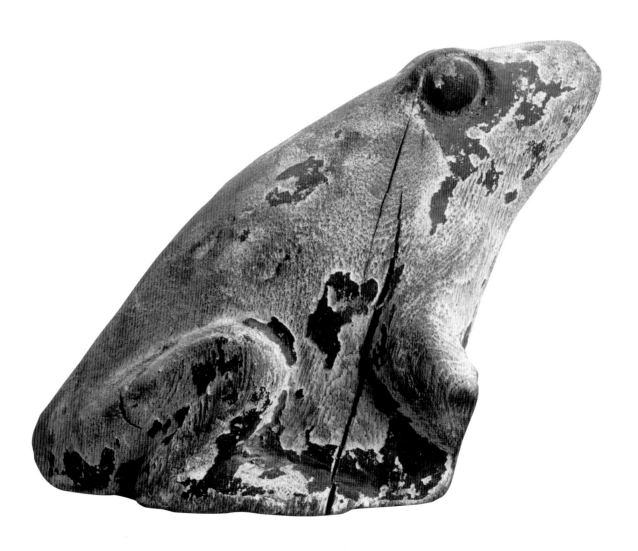

III

The Frog: from Protohistory to the Christian Church

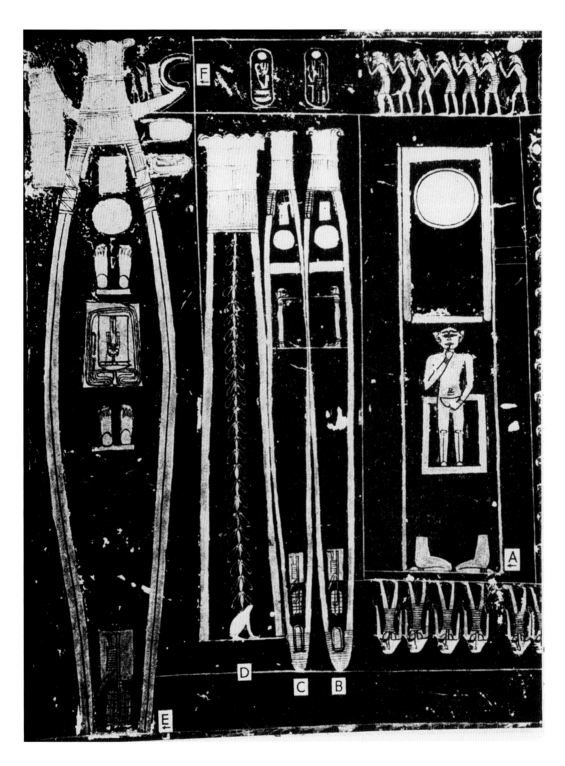

In the Late Period, the small green Egyptian frog started appearing in art produced on the banks of the Nile. Jars were made in frog shapes, their openings fitted into the amphibian's back. The recipients were often small and their contents used to celebrate rituals, probably linked to the theme of rebirth. They were also the prototype for the oil lamp.

REPRESENTATION

At the start of the Old Kingdom, when funerary chapels were built above underground burial chambers, the inside walls of the edifice featured decors representing agrarian life. There was always one scene that took place in the swampland by the river. Against a papyri background, the owner of the tomb was depicted surrounded by his family, hunting and fishing from a light sailing vessel made of reeds or papyrus, reminiscent of primitive boats.

THE WATER CONTEXT

This scene was so often depicted on the walls of funerary chapels throughout the Pharaonic civilization that it has

Miniature funerary figurines
This Predynastic set of miniatures apparently consisted of a she-dog, representing the star Sothis, a hawk in flight, representing Horus, and a frog. Images of Horus and Seth are present on the belly of a small vase. The frog was not an exclusively royal symbol and was also part of the "public" domain, used to express all aspirations for rebirth.
Stone, Predynastic Period, Musée du Louvre, Paris

FACING PAGE:
Frog between two solar barks
The decorations on the ceilings of royal tombs sometimes depicted a small frog suspended on a long stem between the twin images of the Barks of Day and Night. The frog's presence helped the sun's journey between the two vessels.
Royal tomb, New Kingdom, Valley of the Kings, Western Thebes

become a well-known cliché. The common explanation of this scene is that it depicts the deceased relaxing by practising his favorite sport in the afterlife. As a form of relaxation, however, it would have become monotonous for a whole eternity; all the deceased had to do was spear two fish from the water and kill wild ducks with a stick.

This familiar scene in fact represents a noble building up his reserves of food for eternity, but this is not all. His hunting and fishing occupations have more to do with the difficulties of the afterlife, as we shall see.

Lurking far from the boatman at the bottom of the water is a hippopotamus that the deceased has to avoid. However, the hippopotamus is shown being attacked by another demon incarnation, the crocodile. It is effectively the struggle between the two monsters that will protect the transformation of the newly dead.

In the papyrus undergrowth, there is an extensive bestiary: a light locust on a reed, an *ichneumon* ("Pharaoh's rat") watching the nesting birds, a butterfly ready to land on a leaf, and at the heart of this activity, calmly sitting on a succulent plant, is the placid frog. From the position of the amphibian, it seems to be guiding the postmortem boat along its desired path to ensure the deceased's passage to light and eternity.

IN THE BIRTHING CHAMBER

The frog also lent its countenance to the feminine spirit that presides over births. In scenes depicting theogamy on the walls of New Kingdom temples, it appeared in this guise to illustrate the birth of the child begotten to the queen and god. Heket, the divinity with a woman's body and frog's head, is represented at the birth of the future Queen Hatshepsut, and that of the future Amenhotep III.

A POWERFUL FORCE OF RENAISSANCE

Objects of the civil funeral service may also have had frog decorations to encourage rebirth after death. Furthermore, small T-shaped cups were used for libations after death. The shape of the object was intended to evoke the section of water leading from a river to a landing stage. The use of the

FACING PAGE:
Drinking vessel
This small vessel is decorated with several symbols. Its T-shape is symbolic of safe arrival after a long journey. The lotus, symbol of solar rebirth, sits on the inside edge of a pool containing two *inet* fish, embodying the "soul of yesterday and tomorrow." To ensure a successful rebirth, the small frog watches over the libation as it leaves the receptacle.
Schist,
Eighteenth dynasty,
Musée du Louvre, Paris

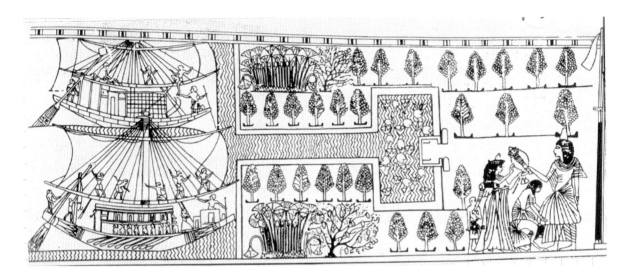

**Port of the temple
of Karnak**
This painting in a Theban
tomb depicts a safe arrival
after the journey to rebirth.
The T-shaped pool represents
a harbor where boats take
shelter.
Tomb of Neferhotep,
Eighteenth dynasty,
Western Thebes

Small wooden frog
Religious object.

cup ensured the owner's safe arrival after a long journey
through the darkness of the underworld. The cup was often
placed among other gifts on a table and adorned with
symbolic decorations to increase its effectiveness. The
Louvre in Paris has a remarkable example of one of these
cups. The interior sides of the recipient are engraved with
images of lotuses, suggesting the appearance of sunlight; the
bottom of the cup is decorated with the two fish,
representing rebirth. To make the ritual liquid even more
effective, the channel through which the water passed was
capped with a minuscule rounded sculpture of a frog.

THE FROG'S APPEARANCE

As a guarantee of entry to the afterlife, the frog was not
overlooked by Queen Nefertari, the principal wife of
Ramses II, when she made her own application for entry to
eternity. In the final room of her burial chamber in the
Valley of the Queens, at the end of her ascent from
darkness, the sovereign is seen standing before the ibis-
beaked god Thoth, master of the calendar, flood, and divine
speech. To obtain the assistance essential for her ultimate
transformation, the queen presents him with a scribe's
palette and the image of a majestic frog standing on its hind

legs. This gesture will enable the queen to master the magic writings and, through the work of the frog, obtain a passage to the light in the world of eternity.

Whenever the theme of rebirth was evoked, the frog always had its place in the Egyptian figurative landscape. In the temple of Dendara, at the time of the seventh Cleopatra, priests created a detailed representation of Osiris' burial chamber, the god who would ensure greater hope of survival in the afterlife. They made sure to place the frog, Heket, close to Osiris' mummy, and not far from Isis and Nephthys, the two goddess-guardians responsible for the recomposition of the divine body. The frog is depicted sitting peacefully near the bed where Osiris's mummy lies, thus guaranteeing his anticipated rebirth when Nature reawakens. Germination

Sety I in adoration of the frog
This divine spirit is the frog Heket. Sety I dedicated a chapel to Heket in his temple, where he came to pray for good Osirian fortune and survival in the afterlife.
Temple of Sety I, Nineteenth dynasty, Abydos

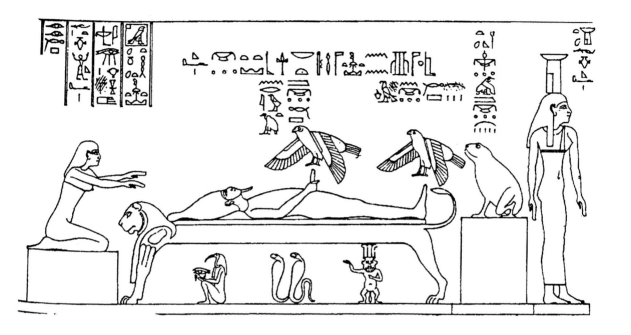

The funerary bed of Osiris
Isis, the great magician, in the form of a bird, descends on the body of the mummified Osiris to impregnate herself. On the right is the frog spirit, Heket, expressing desire for the rebirth of the posthumous heir, Horus.
Temple of Isis, Greco-Roman Period, Island of Philae

FACING PAGE:
The frog of Nefertari
Ramses II himself probably supervised the creation of the masterpieces decorating the tomb of his beloved wife. The queen presents the frog to the master of writing and the calendar, Thoth, so as to obtain a happy rebirth. The scribe's palette is a homage to the divine intelligence of Thoth.
Tomb of Nefertari, Nineteenth dynasty, Valley of the Queens

is symbolized by the ithyphallic appearance of the martyr god on which Isis, the bird, will land to be impregnated. Another representation in Philae shows Isis approaching the body of her revived husband. There is a frog, perched by the divine bed, looking on.

THE FROG, THE ETERNAL ACCESSORY OF WORSHIP

When the last fires of pagan Egypt were going out and the Emperor Justinian had ordered worshippers to abandon the last temple of Egypt on the island of Philae, Christianity had already spread through the land of Isis, whose heritage it had subsumed. In the new places of worship, Isis was depicted enthroned, holding a child-god to his breast; elderly Egyptians would have readily recognized the child Horus.

The religion continued to be worshipped, bathed in the fragrances of incense and frankincense from Punt, "land of the god," by the glow of small oil lamps in the shape of a frog, the eternal guardian of life.

IV

Fish, Taboos, and Resurrection

Taboos

Among the fish to inhabit the old Nile, the Oxyrhynchus (*Mormyrus*) had a certain demonic renown. According to legend, it swallowed the phallus of Osiris, the god martyr, after his brother Seth had killed him, cut him into pieces, and thrown him in the river.

THE NILE TILAPIA AND NILE PERCH

There were two other succulent Nile inhabitants that were not always first choice on the menu for Egyptians, because some regions in the country considered them taboo. Writings forbade people from eating them. The first was a kind of breamlike fish, with pink fins and modest proportions. Today, it has been identified as a species of *Tilapia*. Today known as a *bolti*, in ancient Egypt it was called *inet*.

Unlike the tilapia, the Nile perch *(Lates niloticus)* could and can still reach the size of a man. It was sometimes confused with the legendary fish *abdju*, which made it part of the Osiris myth. It was a fish cloaked in mystery, and one of its essential aspects was revealed by a wall painting in a burial chamber in Deir el-Medina. We see a large fish represented on a funerary

**The most
popular fish in Egypt**
Appreciated for the quality of its flesh, the small *Tilapia nilotica* was also a symbol of resurrection. In ancient Egypt, the Nile tilapia was known as *inet*; today it is called *bolti*.
Glazed terra cotta slab, Nineteenth dynasty, Egyptian Museum, Cairo

FACING PAGE:
Detail from the mystical fishing scene of Menna
Small details make it possible to distinguish the two fish.

**The deceased
in the form of a fish**
In the deceased's first
transformation, he is plunged
into the primal water and
takes the form of the
legendary fish, *abdju*. He takes
on the appearance of the *Lates
niloticus*, or Nile perch, here
mummified under the
protection of the dog-headed
Anubis.
Theban tomb,
Nineteenth dynasty,
Western Thebes

bed, surrounded by the two goddesses of the resurrection of the
dead, Isis and Nephthys, as well as Anubis, leaning over the
fish's heart, in human mummy form. The scene depicts the
deceased's first transformation, receiving the funerary rights
that will lead him to the primordial waters in his quest for
eternity.

It appears that the two fish, the tilapia and perch, were used
as images to illustrate two essential stages of the multiple
changes involved in death. Their presence meant that such
funerary customs became attached to the legend of Osiris
spreading throughout the country. The evil Seth had twice used
the Nile to make his brother disappear, and twice Osiris' body
resisted destruction.

THE TILAPIA, OR INET

I had never had the chance to consider the significance of the
two fish (nor had they aroused the curiosity of my colleagues)
until the day I absolutely had to understand the significance of
their presence on a small jar I had acquired for the Louvre in

Inet ready for resurrection
Two spirits of the flood
prepare the deceased for
resurrection by giving life to
the small *inet* fish that will
convey the deceased's soul.
Enameled schist,
Eighteenth dynasty,
Musée du Louvre, Paris

PRECEDING PAGES:
The mystical hunting and fishing scene of Menna
This classical scene existed from the Old Kingdom onward, supplemented with additional details up to the Late Period. The finest example decorates the burial chamber of Menna. For more than a century, the scene has been interpreted as a representation of the deceased fishing. In reality, the scene depicts the deceased's efforts to retrieve his "soul of yesterday and tomorrow."
Tomb of Menna,
Eighteenth dynasty,
Western Thebes

A miracle catch
The two fish, *inet* and *abdju*, barely distinguishable, are captured by the deceased, who thus takes possession of his "soul of yesterday and tomorrow."
Tomb in Saqqara,
Fifth dynasty

Paris. The image of the tilapia is engraved on this jar, flanked by two crouching anthropomorphic representations of the flood. By the position of one of the hands of the figures, they appear to be protecting the fish.

My research into the two fish returned to the famous swampland "hunting and fishing" scene decorating virtually all funerary chapels throughout ancient Egyptian times.

Fishing Scenes

We know that, from the Old Kingdom onward, chapel walls were illustrated by papyri and reed boats symbolic of the boat used by the deceased to enjoy his fantastical hunting and fishing trip. In these scenes, in front of the boat's prow, a section of water appears to have been raised above the level of the river in order to reveal the two fish, the tilapia and perch, speared by the dead man. The spearing of the perch would ensure the perennial form of his mortal frame, while the tilapia ensured his future. The fish effectively represented the limits of his journey to the afterlife. The slightly bloated shape of the tilapia sometimes contrasts with the long form of the perch.

By the time we reach the walls of the Theban tombs of the New Kingdom, the two fish are only very rarely differentiated, although their own meanings are clear. For a long time, this scene was interpreted as the deceased's preferred form of relaxation, his family pastime in the afterlife. This explanation is now considered erroneous, partly because of the unrealistic nature of the representation: the man is standing on a boat that is too small, and is escorted by his family in festive regalia. His wife is dressed in her finest attire and wears jewelry ill suited to an outdoor sporting scene. Furthermore, the deceased is represented twice on the boat, first as a fisherman, spearing sacred fish from the water, and secondly as a hunter using a stick (not a boomerang!) to break the necks of wild swampland ducks, the symbols of the demons that might assail him during the ritual required to transport him safely from death to survival, on the journey to the eternal light of the sun.

THE REFUGE OF THE SOUL

For the righteous, the fishing and hunting scene was an essential passport to eternal happiness and a guarantee of their access to it. Egyptians' florid imaginations brought a number of

Fishing scene
In this variation, the deceased, using a double line, gallantly catches two fish for his wife and two for himself. The scene takes place during the period when the flood arrives, indicated by the ripe vine ready for harvest.
Theban tomb, Nineteenth dynasty, Western Thebes

Swimmer and *inet*
This bucolic scene must really represent the deceased swimming in the primal waters into which death has plunged her. To attain eternity, she has to retrieve the *inet* fish.
Artist's study, Eighteenth dynasty

**The resurrection
of the soul**

Thoth, master of the calendar,
brings back to eternal life the
soul of the deceased, which
has taken the form of the
inet fish.

Mythological papyrus,
Late New Kingdom,
Egyptian Museum, Cairo

variations to the scene, the most original of which is a scene
where the deceased, sitting near his wife, is seen fishing two of
the same fish, both tilapias, with a double line. He then casts
his double line and catch over his shoulder to gallantly offer
both fish to his wife. Then he uses the same system to hook the
same catch. The scene is supplemented by the T-shaped pool of
the landing stage that welcomes the new waters of regeneration
on New Year's Day. Nearby we also notice the image of the
vine, heavy with grapes, ripening at the start of the flood, the
symbol of the glory of the renascent Osiris.

Two small tilapias, attached to the same line, were later used
to express this same idea of preparation for transformation in
the afterlife, according to the deceased's earthly deeds. The fish
are depicted attached to a single line and became the second
sign of the Egyptian zodiac, illustrating the covers of Greco-
Roman sarcophaguses in Egypt. From these sarcophaguses,
theories of other symbols used to express the transformations of
the dead were developed (see chapter 1).

These two fish, still on the same line, also constitute the
second sign of the zodiac surrounding the impressive image of
Christ, majestically enthroned over the basilica of La
Madeleine in Vézelay, in central France. This zodiac was
copied from the later symbols for the twelve months of the
Egyptian calendar (see chapter 14).

THE FISH OF CHRISTIANITY

Excavations of the monastic cells (*kellia*) dating from the early centuries AD in the desert southeast of Alexandria have revealed images of the fish, the sign of the new faith, and that of Christ the Savior. One example, drawn by a monk on a cell wall, is now conserved in the Coptic section of the Department of Egyptian Antiquities at the Musée du Louvre in Paris. On it one can clearly make out the fish dominated by a cross.

The fish is at the origin of the word *ichthys*, the monogram emblem of the early Christians of Egypt. The word is shorthand for "Jesus Christ, son of God the Savior": *Iesous Christos Theou Yios Soter.*

EXCURSUS

Traces of customs and beliefs from Pharaonic times survive in modern Egypt in the remotest regions. In the south of Aswan, in the heart of beautiful Nubia, once miles from any city and now submerged by the waters of Lake Nasser, I was able to witness the continuation of these beliefs, in particular the myth of the tilapia as the refuge of the soul after death. At the time, we were trying to save a series of temples that had been submerged for long months in the waters of the first Aswan dam. In the summer, the sluice gates of the former dam were opened, and the Ptolemaic temples along the banks of the Nile in the region were emptied of water, including the sanctuary of the Nubian god Mandulis in Kalabsha.

We were working not far away on a large Nilometer well, built into the huge passageway surrounding the temple. The Egyptian Antiquities Service had very kindly responded to our request for an on-site doctor during the mission over the summer months, when work accidents and snakebites are more prevalent.

Fate smiled on us, however, and there were no unfortunate incidents. The doctor had nothing to do and grew bored. So, he decided to go fishing in the deep waters of the sacred well to catch *inets* with their succulent flesh. He had not counted on our Nubian workers who, realizing the doctor's intentions, hurried over to him shouting these words that remain engraved in my memory: "Stop! You're mad! You're not going to eat our ancestors!"

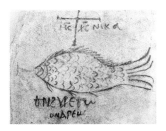

The fate of the *inet* fish
Graffiti in a monastic cell
Musée du Louvre, Paris

V

The Game of Goose
and the Greeks

THE GOOSE OF THE NILE

Popular in Europe during the Renaissance, the game of goose is rather a curiosity among board games today, but retains a cult status in its local varieties across Europe. We have to go way back in time, several millennia, to the banks of the Nile to discover the game's origins. The game of goose was a typically Egyptian game, the aim of which is obvious: to enable the goose of Amun, the Egyptian goose (*Chenalopex*), which migrates the length of Africa from Cairo to the Cape, to free the sun from darkness.

THE ORIGIN OF THE GAME

It seems the game first appeared in its definitive form before the first dynasty, when hieroglyphics were in the early stages of development. There are still some examples of game boards from the first dynasty, of which the best conserved specimens can be found at the Leyden Museum in the Netherlands and the Louvre in Paris. The Louvre example was carved in calcite and is a circular tray twenty-seven inches in diameter, fitted with a curved base to form a kind of low table.

The goose of Amun
The migrating Egyptian goose flies from the mouth of the river to its source, where Amun was born.
Stuccoed wood and bronze,
Late New Kingdom,
Musée du Louvre, Paris

FACING PAGE:
Young girl with gosling
The girl, holding a gosling, will reappear in the gosling's image for her solar rebirth.
Tomb painting,
Eighteenth dynasty,
Western Thebes

BELOW, LEFT:
Detail of the goose's head
For the person who wins the game, the sun will emerge from the head of the goose on the side of the *mehen* snake's coiled body.
Musée du Louvre, Paris

BELOW, RIGHT:
The game of goose
Game board in the form of the coiled body of the *mehen* snake. At the edge, the goose's head appears ready to "spit out" the sun. In the center, the snake's tongue is visible, darting out to ward off enemies of the daystar.
Alabaster, First dynasty,
Musée du Louvre, Paris

Illustrations from the Old Kingdom on the walls of the Giza or Saqqara funerary chapels show scenes depicting the game of goose, where two men are shown sitting on the ground on each side of the table. For daily use, the board was made of terracotta, but when included in funerary furnishings, the table was fashioned from more durable materials such as stone.

The game was composed of a stable board and counters, as well as jacks or short two-sided sticks essential for moving the counters backwards, forwards, or nowhere.

THE SNAKE

The general layout of the board resembles the one used for game of goose. The starting point is at the head of a long thin curled snake in the center of the board. The snake's eyes are wide open and staring, and its tongue is sticking out, a well-known prophylactic gesture. The folds of the snake are decorated by an uninterrupted series of small boxes, sometimes decorated by small painted vignettes, which illustrate an adventure made up of good fortune and setbacks, the worst of which for the player is the well. At the end of the trail, outside the final fold at the reptile's tail, appears the goose's head with its distinctive beak.

Snakes are common on Egypt's baked earth and naturally feature in the ancient Egyptian symbolic bestiary. Not all

have fatal bites like the cobra, which was considered so majestically dangerous that it was accorded the role of defender of the crown. The most poisonous was the horned viper (*Cerastes cerastes*), the bite of which was still fatal fifty years ago. The snake in the game of goose was clearly not the horned viper, whose head was equipped with a kind of diadem of small rough points; besides, the horned viper is a gray-green invertebrate the size of a large slug, too small for the game. The game's serpent was instead a mythical snake, the *mehen*, a huge creature which would mark out the trail of the deceased's meanderings when they undertook their journey to their desired eternity.

In the tombs of the Valley of the Kings, the nighttime journey of the sun is evocative of the deceased's journey in his bark, protected by the coiled *mehen* who enfolds his ram-headed human form.

In the tombs of the Valley of the Kings, this voyage is symbolized by the nocturnal journey of the sun on its boat, protected by the *mehen* surrounding coiling around its human body with a ram's head.

For the deceased, eternity would finally be revealed when, in his transformation, he finally fused with dazzling light. After surmounting multiple obstacles on the way, and passing the twelve doors or caverns of the night (to which Dante later alludes), the miracle is complete. The solar goose could then give birth to its gosling, the revived star.

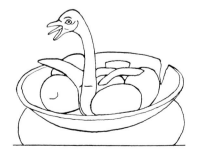

THE SOLAR GOOSE AND CREATION

Again the ancient Egyptians deployed their device of expressing straightforward ideas through multiple symbols.

The gander might well be able to "cackle" about Creation but, in a country where domestic fowl were not bred, the goose's role was to brood the egg of Creation. It is not surprising therefore to find the relief image of a chirping gosling surrounded by eggs decorating the lid of an ointment jar in Tutankhamun's treasure; the young goose's kindly magical influence would ensure the king's awakening. The solar gosling associated with a royal prince is so common an image that the bird is sometimes depicted flying over the representation of the child king, whereas that of the adult sovereign is protected by the vulture.

Back in mortal life, winning the game would ensure success and prosperity. And when it came to the journey into the kingdom of Osiris, the magical game had to be included in the deceased's funerary equipment to help earn a place beside the Creator. We shall return to this later.

THE IMPORTANCE OF ACCESSORIES

The game of goose was clearly the most popular game along the banks of the Nile and it survived for thousands of years. Its counters were customized, either marked with the name of each player or modeled differently, so as to tell the difference between players. The owner of the game might use a sphinx; his opponent that of the foreign counter to distinguish the adversaries.

The Louvre conserves a small counter, which dates back to the first dynasty and is shaped like a house with a double-sloped roof, a feature of dwellings in in climes where rainfall was frequent, such as the region now known as Lebanon for example.

Much later, in the New Kingdom, dignitaries used counters with dual circular faces made of ivory, engraved with the name of their holder. There were also small counters, terra cotta discs enameled in different colors, used as a base for lucky animals, including the cheetah; there were others used as a base for Asian or African prisoners, hands tied behind their back, a posture that naturally limits the subject's movement.

Tutankhamun's earring
The young prince's jewelry had to include the image of a vulture, the symbol of the king. On closer inspection, we see that the head of the vulture has been replaced by that of a gosling.
Gold and transparent blue glass, Eighteenth dynasty, Egyptian Museum, Cairo

FACING PAGE:
The great royal nurse holding her infant prince
On the lap of the royal nurse is the future Amenophis II. The prince's youth is emphasized by the bird flying overhead, which is depicted, not with a vulture's head, but as a vulture with the head of the divine gosling.
Theban tomb, Eighteenth dynasty, Western Thebes

"House" game piece
The game of *senet* was always included among funerary equipment to help the deceased overcome demons in his passage to the other world. To allude to these demons, the Egyptian fashioned their game pieces in the shape of houses with roofs of a different shape to those in Egypt.
Ivory, First dynasty,
Musée du Louvre, Paris

**Game piece
in the form of a lion**
The owner of this terrifying piece could always hope to win the game.
Ivory, First dynasty,
Musée du Louvre, Paris

THE SYMBOL OF THE CHEETAH

When studying the Egyptian bestiary, I realized that ancient Egypt never used animals foreign to its territory as lucky symbols with the exception of the cheetah. This long-necked cat with its non-retracting claws, round ears, and huge dark fur "tears" beneath its eyes was familiar to the early Egyptians. At the dawn of history, it appeared on palettes used in rituals, and in the Middle Kingdom on "magic ivories," as a quadruped with an unfeasibly long neck, protecting a central cupule, the recipient of something precious. Magical allusions to the cheetah decorated accessories, particularly in royal palaces; the golden hip belt belonging to Dahshur's princely treasures (Middle Kingdom) is a magnificent example of this. The belt was intended for protection against disease, a quality ensured by a series of cheetah heads; in descriptions, this creature has often been mistaken for a leopard. Later in the New Kingdom, the cheetah's head was used to transmit its protective strength to the king's ceremonial loincloth.

The cheetah, a hunter of electric pace, was said to come from the legendary land of Punt (the "land of the god") situated between Sudan and Ethiopia. It is no surprise to learn that, on a New Kingdom expedition to the country, Queen Hatshepsut brought back a pair of cheetahs from the land of Amun, who "never left her side." The animals were

worthy additions to the royal menagerie. Today, in Basel Museum, there is a beautiful small bloodstone cheetah head, which was a royal playing counter marked with the name and title of Queen Hatshepsut. Using such a fine piece, no sovereign could fail to win a game gloriously and quickly.

Set of game pieces
Pieces came in all kinds of shapes. The most refined were those inscribed with the name of their owner.
Ivory, First dynasty,
Musée du Louvre, Paris

THE MULTIPLE VARIATIONS OF THE GAME OF GOOSE

Over the course of the New Kingdom, the game of goose underwent several variations and simplifications. It sometimes abandoned the initial appearance of the snake, on which its form was based, and it can be traced to England where it is known as "snakes and ladders." It was adopted by other countries with practically no changes, but the snake's head was switched for that of the goose. The table board was reduced to a two-sided mainly wooden box, with a series of thirty squares on one side. One square featured three water signs, recalling the famous well of the game of goose. On the other side of the box, there were even fewer squares in a similar arrangement to the boxes in the game of hopscotch.

The game was also reduced to thirty squares, a version known as *senet*, a name that referred to the idea of passage; fitting indeed, as the game was used to ease the passage through the tortuous dark world into which the dead were led. Some rare, unfortunately incomplete texts attest to the fact that its use was also chthonian.

Game of *senet*
The game of *senet* is played on a grid of thirty squares. *Senet* means "passage" and the game provided the means to gain access to the afterlife.
Treasure of Tutankhamun,
Eighteenth dynasty,
Egyptian Museum, Cairo

NEFERTARI, ANDRÉ MALRAUX,
AND THE GAME OF *SENET*

I once had the pleasure of showing André Malraux, then minister of culture, the most beautiful tomb of the Valley of the Queens, that of Queen Nefertari, the principal wife of Ramses II. The writer was stopped in his tracks by the magnificent burial chamber paintings showing the queen sitting beneath a bower made of papyrus stalks, busy playing *senet*. "She's not playing against anybody!" he exclaimed. "Indeed, minister," I replied. "She now lives in the invisible world of the disembodied. Here she has returned to the primordial waters, suggested by the papyrus shelter under which she is sitting. To continue her journey, she has to confront invisible adversaries. Here we see her in action."

André Malraux was a man with a great sense of mysticism. He was very struck by this unexpected meaning and its intense poetic symbolism and could not tear himself from the scene. It was a moment he even talked about shortly before his death, so affected had he been.

FROM HOPSCOTCH TO PENTECOST

For several thousand years there was no game more popular than the game of goose. Each strata of society transformed, interpreted, and exploited it in their own way and the game often changed appearance. One of its metamorphoses in Europe was the game of hopscotch, where the child hops from square to square, pushing quoits from the "Hell" zone to the "Heaven" zone. The aim of the game is still to reach the sun and light.

In cathedrals at Pentecost, priests would also aim for the triumph of the victorious sun when they played their ritual game of real tennis in the cathedral. At Bayou Cathedral, meanwhile, there is a relief sculpture of the game of goose on the floor of the chapterhouse. Indeed, the game never lost its initial circular *mehen* shape, existing to this day as the game of goose, the Nile goose, which holds within it the history of Egypt's journey to attain sunlight.

Nefertari playing *senet*
The principal wife and favorite of Ramses II is represented in the papyrus thickets on the edge of the primal ocean. The setting is suggested by the papyrus-stem tent protecting her.
Painting, tomb of Nefertari, Nineteenth dynasty, Valley of the Queens, Western Thebes

VI

Saint George
and Saint Christopher

Both fortune-bearing figures of Saint George and Saint Christopher come to us from ancient Egypt. Even the country's occupiers, especially the Romans, worshipped the figures, and they were subsequently adopted in Europe due to their concordance with our way of thinking. Adoption was made easier by the way they were gradually adapted as they were passed on. They came to be identified with local heroes, which made them more familiar. However, in many cases, it would not be possible to grasp their deep meaning without understanding more fundamental aspects of their evolution. Here I present two very typical cases.

FACING PAGE:
Detail of a painted canvas representing death and resurrection.
Roman Era,
Musée du Louvre, Paris

Saint George
FROM THE HARPOON KING
TO HORUS THE LEGIONARY

What image could be easier to interpret than that of Saint George on horseback slaying the dragon? The legend originally spread from the east, in all directions westward. From Ethiopia to Russia, the image was the same. In England, Saint George

Tutankhamun with harpoon
The young king is depicted harpoon in hand, in the process of attacking the Nile hippopotamus. His primitive vessel is no more than a papyrus skiff, a reminder of how simple early boats were.
Treasure of Tutankhamun, Eighteenth dynasty, Egyptian Museum, Cairo

FACING PAGE:
Capture of the hippopotamus (detail)
The eternal battle between Horus and Seth (the hippopotamus) injects action into a chapter from the Osiris legend. To accentuate the evil nature of the hippopotamus, the creature's feet have been reduced in size. Horus and his companions harpoon the beast, while the divine mother, Isis, enchains it.
Relief from the temple at Edfu, Greco-Roman Period

even became the country's patron saint. However, all experts concur that legends concerning Saint George have been extremely exaggerated.

THE CLASSICAL LEGEND

For some, the legend of George originates in the ancient Greek world. Near the town of Silena in Libya there once lived a monster for which the population had to sacrifice goats. Its victims then became young boys and girls, including the king's daughter, whom George encounters on her way to being sacrificed. George tackles the mighty beast and lances it. He asks the princess to attach her belt round the beast's neck and the creature is led back like a tame dog.

Other legends state that George was born in Cappadocia around AD 303. A wealthy noble, he entered the imperial army, destroying many an idol. Arrested by Diocletian, he was martyred three times in seven years and buried in Lydda in Palestine, in a special basilica where Tel Aviv now stands.

It is not hard to see from these examples the central role the Romans played in passing on legends and transforming them and their original themes.

HORUS, THE HARPOON KING

Back in the eighteenth dynasty (the mid-fourteenth century BC), in the funerary inventory of the young king Tutankhamun, we find the elegant gold painted wooden figurine of the young sovereign standing on a light vessel casting a harpoon. The gesture, oft repeated on the banks of the Nile, recalls the age-old image of a chief overcoming a crocodile or a hippopotamus lurking at the bottom of the river.

More than thirteen centuries later, on one of the walls in the Ptolemaic temple at Edfu devoted to Horus the solar hawk, we find another image that echoes this magical composition. This time, in heroic human form with the head of a hawk, we find Horus by his riverboat attacking a hippopotamus with his long harpoon, driving the beast back into the water. The smallness of the beast in comparison with the god highlights the power of Horus, the slayer of harmful beasts, and protector who destroys evil.

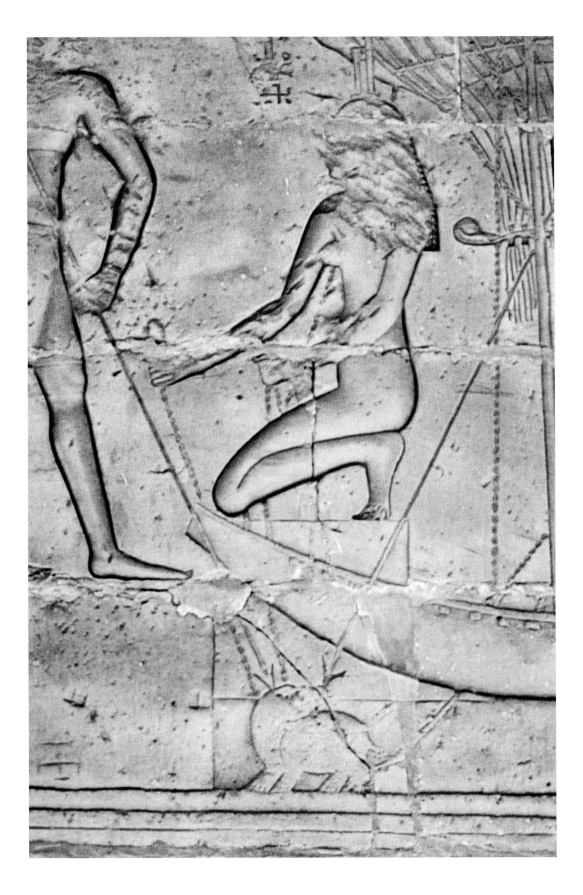

Saint George
Horus was transformed into a
classic Saint George,
acquiring a human form
depicted slaying the dragon,
depending on the artist's
imagination.
Mosaic inlaid in wood,
Fourteenth century,
Byzantium

FACING PAGE:
Horus the legionary
We have found a providential
transitional image from the
Roman era, in which "Horus
the savior" appears dressed as
a Roman legionary on
horseback. Horus is clearly
recognizable by his hawk's
head. The hippopotamus is
replaced by a Nile crocodile.
Relief, Early Coptic Period,
Musée du Louvre, Paris

INTERPRETATION OF THE EGYPTIAN THEME

The Romans picked up on the theme and adapted it to create a composite image, an accessible compromise for both occupied and occupiers. In some of these, the monster to be destroyed is transformed into a large crocodile while the victor maintains his human form. Only the hawk's head recalls the victor's original divine identity, having replaced that of the sovereign. To overwhelm his enemy, Horus is no longer standing on his boat but, like a Roman legionary, is portrayed on horseback, out of the question for Egyptians. We are fortunate enough at the Louvre to possess a Coptic image of this transition, representing a Roman rider with a hawk's head killing the demon, a crocodile. Even the iconography of Saint Sisinius in Ethiopia perpetuated this image of solar Horus destroying evil.

We encounter this age-old theme from Byzantium to Russia, passing through western Europe where, everywhere, the Nile monster was replaced by a dragon.

Saint Christopher
ANUBIS AND THE PATRON SAINT OF TRAVELERS

The origins of Saint Christopher are to be found in the figure of Anubis as the patron god of travelers. But they are by no means as easy to identify as the origins of Saint George.

THE LEGEND OF SAINT CHRISTOPHER

Saint Christopher is a figure of many legends, some of which are quite surprising. In some, he was born in the ancient Greek world, near Silena in Libya. However, Jacobus de Voragine's *Golden Legend* presents Christopher as a kindly giant, twelve cubits tall, a native of the land of Canaan.

Christopher first enters the service of the most powerful king in the world. Having heard say, by the king himself, that the devil is more powerful than his sovereign, Christopher sets out after the devil and journeys with him through the desert. Suddenly a cross appears and the devil takes flight. Caught by Christopher, the devil tells him that Christ is even more powerful than himself. Christopher sets off in search of Christ, and encounters a hermit who baptizes him and recommends

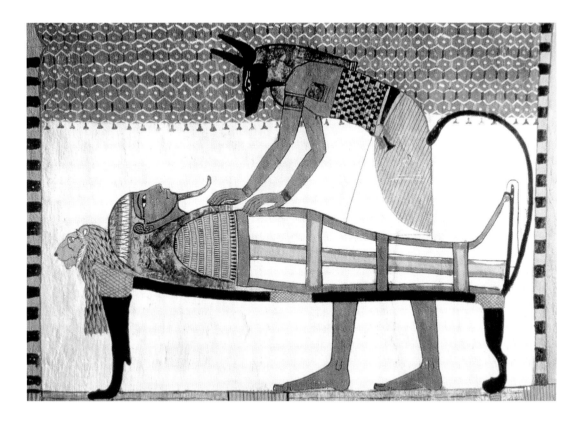

that he fast, but Christopher cannot maintain his fast. The hermit then advises the kindly giant to recite prayers, but Christopher muddles the words. Finally, the hermit takes him to a fast-flowing river where, every year, many travelers are drowned. Christopher lifts the travelers onto his back and crosses the raging waters, with his stick as a guide.

One day, he leaves his shelter to answer the call of a child. He places the child on his shoulders and starts to cross the river. In the middle of the river, the child has become so heavy that the giant, bent double, has trouble progressing. On the other riverbank, he asks the child who he is. "You were a burden so heavy it was as though I was carrying the world on my shoulders," he says. "Don't be surprised, Christopher," replied the child, "for upon your shoulders you have not only carried the entire world, but the creator of that world. I am Jesus Christ." Then the child disappears. Suddenly Christopher notices that his stick planted in the sand is now covered in leaves and flowers.

**Anubis watches
over the mummy**
Because of the pose of this god with a dog's head (not that of a jackal), Anubis was long thought to have assisted Isis with the mummification of Osiris. However, this seems to not to be the case. Anubis, standing by the mummy, seems to be touching his heart or leading the deceased toward the balance of judgment. In the Late Period, he was thought to be the guide of deceased.
Tomb painting in Deir el-Medina, Nineteenth dynasty

Christopher, a barbarian Christian, reminiscent of Hercules, is a born servant. He enters the Roman army, refuses to renounce his faith, and dies under torture in Samos, Lydia.

THE PROTOTYPE OF SAINT CHRISTOPHER

In ancient Egyptian history, the Christopher prototype is Anubis (*Inpw* in Egyptian), who during a funeral rite appears near Isis leaning over the heart of the mummy Osiris. Near the scales of judgment, he shares the same role as Thoth, calibrating the scales exactly. Anubis is almost constantly depicted by the side of the mummy, which is ready for the journey into the afterlife, and this has led to a common conclusion that the human silhouette with its black dog's head (not that of a jackal) was instrumental in the mummification process. Anubis, after all, helped the widow of Osiris gather her husband's dismembered remains after Seth's violent murder. However, there is no textual evidence for this. When Anubis is mentioned, he is said to be *imiut*,

which means that he is imagined in a kind of animal skin
(*ut*). It is said that he is either *khenty-seh netjer* ("at the head of
the divine pavilion") or *tepy-dju-ef* ("on his hill or mountain").
Only in several cases is Anubis cited as being in the *per nefer*
(meaning "house of mummification" or "house of vitality"),
and thus able to assist Isis.

THE CHAPEL OF DEIR EL-BAHRI

The monument that most helps understand the identity of
Anubis, and one that has not received the attention it merits,
is the great chapel specially dedicated to him in Deir el-Bahri.
In my study of Queen Hatshepsut, I showed that this great
sovereign built, to the north of her mortuary temple,
chambers specially devoted to the transformations undergone
before resurrection she, expressed by the image of herself in
human form with the head of a black dog. This mysterious
temple tells the story of the deceased's journey from darkness
to solar eternity.

**Anubis (*inpw*), guiding and
weighing**
Not only was Anubis
considered to take care of the
balance of judgment for the
deceased, but he was also
depicted as guiding the
deceased to the scales.
Funerary papyrus,
late New Kingdom,
Egyptian Museum, Cairo

Discovery of Anubis in the burial chamber of Tutankhamun
Priests dressed this magnificent life-size statue of the black dog in thick white linen to make it more comfortable in the darkness of the burial chamber. The sculpture was placed in the tomb chamber, facing north, in the company of canopic jars and models of sailing craft.
Treasure of Tutankhamun, Eighteenth dynasty, Egyptian Museum, Cairo

FACING PAGE:
Anubis and Horemheb
Anubis seems to be leading the pharaoh Horemheb from the moment he enters the tomb.
Painting, tomb of Horemheb, Eighteenth dynasty, Valley of the Kings, Western Thebes

ANUBIS–HORUS

In the burial chamber of Tutankhamun there is an inscription on the wall of the East room, dedicated to the "awakening" of the dead. The inscription reads that the king "compared in appearance to Horus." Furthermore, the neck of the statue of the black dog in the tomb is protected, as always, by a long linen scarf, proof that it represents the dead king. The black dog statue is lying on a very high pedestal with the inscription "He is on his mountain." In the layout of the tomb, it replaces the communicating door between the North and East chambers, the destination of the changing king. This reveals the statue is symbolic of a rite of passage.

This representation of a dead king in transition is even indicated by the name *Inpw*, the name given to uncrowned princes or royal heirs the moment before birth.

THE DEAD KING ANUBIS

There are at least three burial chambers in the Valley of the Queens that depict this idea of a dead queen transformed as Anubis. On one of the side walls of the entrance chambers to the tomb of an anonymous queen (no. 40), we see the dog of Anubis on the same pedestal, twice representing the dead queen.

In the tomb of Nefertari, the principal wife of Ramses II, there are two paintings of the black dog lying on his column, on the side wall of the chamber at the base of the staircase leading to the chamber of rebirth.

The most vivid picture is to be found on the upper side wall of the burial chamber of Bent-Anat, elder daughter and wife to Ramses II (tomb no. 71). The queen in the form of a black dog lying on a pylon is at the center of the "opening of mouth and eyes" ceremony. The identification of the dead princess with the image of Anubis is unmistakable.

CIVILIAN DEAD AS ANUBIS

Much later, in the Roman era, when people were more sensitive to the mysteries inherent in the transformations of the deceased, the role of guide was often mixed up with the idea of the spirit that has not yet left the darkness. The guide was represented on decorated shrouds for example as a human body with the head of a black dog, welcoming and accompanying the deceased.

FACING PAGE:

The transformation of the deceased

The deceased was flanked by figures that represent his two essential transformations: on the left, his mummy recalls his ancestral form; on the right, the figure with the black dog's head, sun blazing overhead, symbolizes the invisible transformations he will undergo after death. In the center is the portrait of his eternal resurrection.

Painted canvas,
Roman era,
Musée du Louvre, Paris

Anubis, gatekeeper
This figure of the deceased is carrying keys round his neck to enable him to open the twelve gates of the afterlife.
Fragment of a sarcophagus, Late Period, Valley of the Queens, Western Thebes

FACING PAGE:
Saint Christopher with dog's head
"Christophoros," who visibly "carried Christ," was also invisibly carried by him, according to the tradition of Simeon (Luke 2:25). He who carries Christ is he who traverses hell (symbolized by the dog).
Seventeenth century, Byzantium Museum, Athens

In some cases, Anubis is not really a guide. He is shown arriving at the end of the journey when he has left his form of darkness and has reappeared resurrected.

Ancient Egyptian texts specify that, in the town of Mendes, the dead man, in the guise of Anubis, would take possession of the solar breath of resurrection, as indicated by the solar disc often placed behind the ear of the black dog.

These Egyptian shrouds dating back to the Roman era show the deep and lasting knowledge of Egyptian priests on the subject. One of the most beautiful examples of this type is conserved at the Louvre.

ANUBIS, SHADOW OF THE CIVILIAN DEAD

This same scene appears identically in a number of places, but its real message has never been interpreted until today. The main theme is represented by the central figure of the deceased standing facing forward. He is dressed in Roman white. His mummy, and not the image of Osiris, is standing to his right, wearing the crown of Osiris, and holding in his hands the scepters of god. On the other side, we can see Anubis, as a black dog. His animal head is in profile and a large solar disc appears behind his pert ear. His right hand is lying on the shoulder of the resuscitated deceased, while his left hand is placed on the deceased's chest to both protect him and make him appear.

ANUBIS, THE GUIDE AND FERRYMAN

These ceremonies drew on the legend of Isis and were adopted by the Roman occupiers. In their adapted form, we see the emperor at the head of processions, his chest and face covered with the breastplate and mask of a black dog. In the role of guide accorded the figure later, the head of a dog or baboon was replaced by a human face, that of Saint Christopher, the ferryman.

Thus, Anubis in mutant form conquered the Western world as the protector of travelers.

VII

From Turquoise Mines
to the Alphabet

The Egyptians made numerous expeditions to mines and quarries. These included trips to the Sinai peninsula in search of precious copper and turquoise.

FACING PAGE:
Sinai peninsula,
aerial view.

THE ROAD TO SINAI

Turquoise, a magnificent glowing blue stone, was known throughout the Near East and was worn to bring good luck. It was known as *mefkat* (or *faruz* today) and has been mined at the Serabit el-Khadim and Wadi Maghara sites for nearly four thousand years.

In the Middle Kingdom, workers would leave the Egyptian coast at a point level with Fayum and sail across the Red Sea to the Sinai peninsula. In the New Kingdom, they were able to travel further south, parallel with Thebes, and go via Wadi Hammamat between the Nile and Red Sea. Here they mined gold and graywacke, the famous Bekhen stone. The Wadi Hammamat finally led to the port of Kosseir. Once on the edges of the peninsula, the final stage of the journey led into the heart of the imposing mountain range. The range is a sea of

The rock mountains of Sinai displaying their deep colors. The unusual mountainous landscape of the region seems to have been crafted by human hand.

jostling crests and ridges as far as the eye can see, and the view from its peaks was both grandiose and strange. Its rocks in deep colors are, in places, as though incrusted with transparent stone. Rocky paths used by the Bedouins led the miner though the peaks to the quarries.

A MOTLEY EXPEDITION

Most Bedouins in the region were known for their peaceful nature, and Egyptians took advantage of local expert laborers for the sites. Egyptian expeditions were made up of works managers, mine engineers, guards, supervisors, scribes, accountants, a medical team, sorcerer-healers to cure snakebites, and an interpreter.

The Egyptians would generally employ the same local workers each year. Mining sites were made up of groups of Egyptian masters and Bedouin workers, who seem to have had a good and trusting relationship. Work would take place during winter, when the climate was bearable for both man and the precious turquoise, the handling of which was not a good idea during the hot period.

THE TEMPLE OF HATHOR

As soon as the Egyptians started mining in the area, they
started building chapels, which increased in number over
the dynasties. The impressive temple of the powerful and
beautiful Hathor, goddess of the mines, at Serabit el-
Khadim, was continually expanded between the Middle
Kingdom and New Kingdom. From afar, the temple looks
more like a long, snaking centipede surrounded by huge
walls than it does a traditional place of worship. Unfeasibly
tall stelae covered with hieroglyphs and reliefs mark out the
line of buildings. The columns supporting the capitals
display the human face of the goddess portrayed with cow's
ears as a reference to the original cow, Hathor, mother to
the universe.

For more than three months a year in this grandiose,
austere setting, Bedouins and Egyptians learned to live
together, like and help each other, which helped build
a mutual trust between the two ethnic groups. The result
was an extraordinary adventure for which a modicum of
poetic license will be required to make the story more
concrete.

Sinai
Mountain path leading to the
turquoise mines of Serabit el-
Khadim.

The scribe
Image of the perfect civil
servant, but also the man of
letters who accompanied
expeditions.
Giza,
Musée du Louvre, Paris

Entrance to a turquoise mine.
Serabit el-Khadim, Sinai

FACING PAGE, BOTTOM:
**The ruins of the temple
of Hathor.**

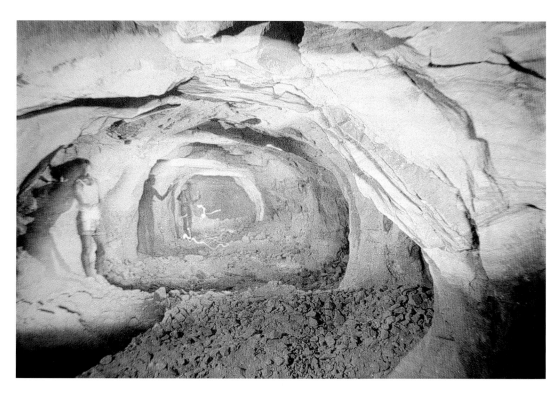

Head of Hathor
A clumsy Bedouin copy
of the Egyptian god Hathor.
Sandstone,
Middle Kingdom,
Serabit el-Khadim

FACING PAGE:
Head of the great Hathor
This is one of the few
Egyptian characters to
be represented face-on.
The cow ears recall the sacred
animal of the divine force
who protected the mines
and quarries.
Gold pendant,
Late New Kingdom

HEALTHY CURIOSITY

At dawn, the men would form groups and take their meals
together, sharing frugal local resources. They made efforts to
get on, assisted by the interpreter, physicians, scribes, and
accountants. The Bedouin inhabitants of the rock desert were
very curious and open-minded. They were intrigued by the
inscriptions covering the walls of the great Hathor's temple, as
well as the lines of hieroglyphics on the high stelae. Who was
this "Lady of the Mountains" called Hathor, who became the
"Mistress of Turquoise"? Early images of the goddess portrayed
her wearing a wide wig with two long locks at the side rolled
into a spiral, not forgetting her cow's ears, a reminder of her
animal origins. In later portraits, she wore her hair more styled,
capped with two elegant cow horns. However, our Bedouin
friends were not just intrigued by the hieroglyphics; they also
wanted to understand them.

Bedouin dinner
After work, Bedouins and
Egyptians would share their
dinner and talk as friends.

THE FIRST LESSON

One evening while dining around the fire, always a
welcoming place in this desert mountain, the most curious
of the young Bedouins asked one of the Egyptian scribes to
draw a few of his intriguing signs on the sand, and explain
what these signs were used for. To the young man's
astonishment, the scribe started explaining with examples:
"Sometimes we draw a sign simply to represent what it depicts
or suggests. So we draw a black viper, so common in the
mountains in the summer, to indicate the snake.
However, most signs also correspond to one or
several sounds and the way they are grouped together
says something very different to their individual meanings,
because they correspond to sounds for writing the Egyptian
language."

COMPARING THE TWO LANGUAGES

When the young Bedouin's initial astonishment had subsided,
he asked the scribe to draw a hieroglyph corresponding to two
sounds. The scribe drew the hieroglyph of a house on the

EGYPT	SINAI	PHOENICIAN	GREEK	PROTO-SINAITIC
maison = *pr*	maison = *b(ei)t* = *b*	A	B	*B a l t*
œil = *ir*	œil = *aïn* = *ā*	A	A	
l = *n+z* =	*lamed (sémitique)* = *l* (sinaï) = *l*	C, V	Λ, Λ	*Hébreux = Baâlat*
(hiéroglyphes)				
(hiératique) =	*tau sémitique* = *t*	X, +	T	*Grecs = Baltis*

Comparative writing table
Table indicating how two Egyptian hieroglyphs were transformed by Bedouins, from the Middle Kingdom in Sinai to Greece and Rome.

Sphinx copied by a Bedouin
There is a Proto-Sinaitic inscription engraved on the base.
Middle Kingdom, Serabit el-Khadim

ground: a rectangle with one of its two sides open in the middle. Others started asking questions:

"What does that mean?"

"How do you pronounce that?"

"It's the outline of a house with an entrance," the scribe replied, "but it can also be the surrounding wall of a house. It is pronounced *per*." (I have simplified things here, because in Egyptian, like other Semitic languages, weak vowels are not written.)

After a moment's thought, the young Bedouin said that his dwelling, his tent, was called *beït*, the same word in Arabic today. He thought again then asked:

"Draw me a new sign."

This time, the scribe drew an eye and told his audience, which had now grown, that it was an eye, as everybody could see.

"In Egyptian, it is pronounced *ir*. What about you?"

"Our word is *ayin*," replied the young man (again the same word in modern Arabic).

Then the scribe finished his demonstration by drawing something resembling a crossroads, which the Bedouin pronounced *taou* (taw) in his language.

Monumental carved hieroglyphs
Here is an example of a magnificent hieroglyphic inscription on a temple wall, in the name of the pharaoh Thutmose III.
Temple of Amada (Nubia), Eighteenth dynasty

A SUGGESTION

"Silence!"

After a moment gathering his thoughts, the young Bedouin declared he would never be able to draw all the scribe's signs to send messages, even though it looked like a good idea.

"In the past, in the hot season," he added, "my father went to work in the lands by the sea [the future Lebanon], far above Egypt; some of us still go there each year. He saw thorn-like signs marked by people on blocks of dried mud [tablets inscribed with cuneiform characters]. The signs don't really have any shape, but apparently these thorns say a lot. I prefer your pictures, but they are very complicated."

THE CREATION OF THE FIRST ALPHABET

The next evening the young Bedouin returned to the fire and told the scribe that he had thought long and hard and he wanted to learn how to write.

"But to draw our language," he added, "we'd need only a few simple signs. If you can help me do this, it would be a gift from god."

So, in the heart of the Sinai desert, the scribe and the young Bedouin, encouraged by their friends, started working through the different signs in their respective languages that might correspond to the sounds they used. It seems they identified thirty or so signs, maybe less. [The following conclusions were drawn from the most convincing work on the subject by Sir Alan Gardiner in the mid-twentieth century.]

The problem for scribe and Bedouin was how to extract the sounds from the words that united them in a single hieroglyph? After several inconclusive efforts, the scribe and Bedouin finally suggested that the sign representing house: ⌐ ⌐ *p(e)r*, translated into the Bedouin's Semitic language by *beït*, could be used to write only the first sound of the word, the letter B. Together they had invented the process of acrophony. Then they started analyzing the second sign, that of an eye: ◁◉▷ , *ir*, pronounced *ayin* in the Bedouin language. According to the same principle of acrophony, they decided to only account for the first letter: A.

They then searched for a word in the Bedouin language that started with BA and decided to try to write the word BALAT, which mean "the Lady," or "supreme mistress," the feminine of

Preparation of papyrus
To make papyrus, the plant was stripped, and the long fibrous strips brushed, before being laid on top of one another at right angles and beaten. Fibers closest to the core of the plant produced the finest paper.
Tomb painting,
Eighteenth dynasty,
Western Thebes

Baal, the Canaanite god. So they searched for an Egyptian word that started with the letter L, but this letter did not exist in Egyptian. So the scribe offered to just take the old Canaanite sound ◡, pronounced *lamed* (which became *lambda* in Greek); written right to left, it appeared as follows: ⊤ .
Finally to right the final T, they drew a △▢◠, which in Egyptian cursive hieratic writing was the simplification of the hieroglyphs △▢◠ used to write T.

Success was theirs! They had managed to write the name of their goddess: Balat!

Then, they went on to select words that started with the different sounds they had identified in the Bedouin language. The scribe found the Egyptian sign corresponding to the one where the opening letter had been retained in its Semitic translation and drew the simplest form. The first Proto-Sinaitic alphabet was born with twenty-five to thirty signs or pictures. It underwent a number of transformations but was finally established between the twelfth and eighteenth dynasties.

THE SPREAD OF THE PROTO-SINAITIC ALPHABET

When exploitation of the turquoise mines ceased, the Bedouin laborers went to find work in the cooler regions of the north (the future Lebanon), where their assistance was greatly appreciated. They took with them their almost magical means of communication, which greatly interested the Canaanites, already familiar with their own complicated cuneiform writing. They went on to adopt these more accessible signs, changing their form slightly with use.

The length of the east coast of the Mediterranean, the Proto-Sinaitic alphabet was used to write different versions of the local languages. It appears certain that the famous alphabet, discovered during excavations of ancient Ugarit, today Ras Shamra, was greatly influenced by the appearance of Proto-Sinaitic writing.

THE ALPHABET'S ODYSSEY

Later, as Plato had anticipated during his research into Phoenician writing, the Greek alphabet became the final development of Proto-Sinaitic writing, inspired as it was by hieroglyphics, and the Hellenes made very intelligent use of it. However, long before classical Greece intervened, illiterate Dorian barbarians invaded Anatolia and moved south to the Peloponnes. Here they made an unexpected linguistic discovery and reaped its rewards; they too modified the signs.

When in the sixth century BC, Potasimto, a Greek general with the Egyptian foreign legion of Psamtik II, took his army to the kingdom of Cush (Sudan) to confront the armies of Aspalta, he passed the two rock-cut temples of Abu Simbel, hollowed into the western bank of the Nubian Nile. Potasimto made sure to record a trace of his passage on the leg of the first southern colossus on the façade of the Ramses temple. This is the first Greek inscription in archaic monumental lettering known to us, and it turns up not in Greece, but in Egypt, bearing signs from the land of Sesostris and Ramses. This alphabet, adopted by the Greeks, was then used by the Romans who were in a good position to introduce it to other countries.

These rudimentary hieroglyphics transformed the way thought was communicated, but using them did not guarantee their transmission. Populations also had to find a support to write on. Up to this point, animal skins, tree bark, fragments of pottery (*ostraca*), wooden boards, and stelae had served had been used, all of which were impractical.

Since the first dynasty, Egypt had been using rolls of papyrus made from the long fibers of the *Cyperus papyrus* plant, which flourished in the swamps of the Nile Delta. The finest fibers on the inside of the stalk were scraped, brushed, beaten, then pressed and stuck together to create two perpendicular layers, made up of sheets ⅙th inch thick, before being rolled up to form *volumen*. Papyrus proved to be a handy way of passing on knowledge and messages. The texts in cursive, hieratic writing were written using fine brushes made from bulrushes. These were dipped into black ink made from ash and gum, or red ink made from desert ruddle, or *gebel*.

Trading in papyrus, the monopoly of the pharaoh, took place with foreign countries via the port of Byblos, in what is now Lebanon, hence the Greek name *biblion* for papyrus. This magnificent medium for thought was used up to the eighth century AD, alongside parchment, before being replaced by rag paper from the East. But the name "papyrus" persisted, with its origins in the Egyptian, *pa* ("the material of") *per aâ* ("the pharaoh")—papyrus.

Papyrus roll
This literary papyrus containing the first "book of dreams" was produced in hieratic signs.
New Kingdom,
Chester Beatty Collection,
Dublin

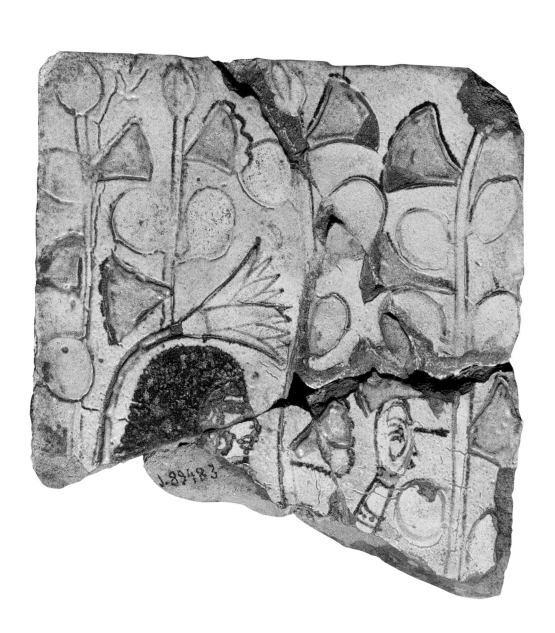

VIII

Egyptian Medicine

THE SON OF IMHOTEP

One of the most ancient and most impressive Egyptian sciences was the art of healing and pharmacopoeia, as practiced by the famous healer Imhotep.

MUMMIFICATION

It is perhaps no surprise that a civilization which, from its very beginnings, strove to preserve the bodies of their deceased from annihilation also invented mummification. So Egypt seems to have been the only Middle Eastern country in ancient times to use the technique that indirectly led them to penetrate the mysteries of the human body.

THE FAME OF *SINW* ABROAD

The reputation of Egyptian physicians, or *sinw*, was such that people came from abroad to consult the secular medics, as opposed to faith healers and sorcerers like the priests of the god Sekhmet or sorcerers of the god Selket.

Inscribed on one of the walls of the Theban tomb of Nebamun, a physician under Amenhotep II's reign, is the

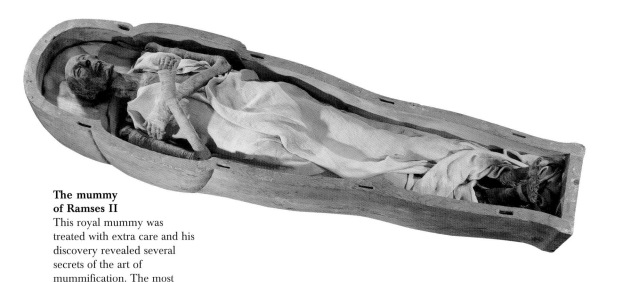

**The mummy
of Ramses II**
This royal mummy was
treated with extra care and his
discovery revealed several
secrets of the art of
mummification. The most
surprising finds emerged
during a medical examination
in Paris, when researchers
found peppercorns in his
nostrils and finely chopped
tobacco leaves in his thorax.

FACING PAGE, TOP:
**Completion of a
mummification**
After the removal of body fat
and organs, except the heart
and kidneys, the deceased's
body was wrapped in linen
strips, then in a shroud, which
was held in place by a
network of overlapping
bandages, as seen here.
Reproduction of an eighteenth
dynasty painting

FACING PAGE, BOTTOM:
**Visit of a Syrian lord
to an Egyptian doctor**
The doctor Nebamun presents
a patient with medication
he has composed himself
following the prescriptions
of his recipe book.
Tomb of Nebamun,
Eighteenth dynasty,
Western Thebes

report of a Syrian prince's visit to consult the great master.
Sporting his luxurious eastern costume and "national" beard, the
prince and his wife form a stark contrast with the physician in his
white linen loincloth. The patient is depicted sitting on an
impressive stool, while his wife, enveloped in a Babylonian-style
multicolored triple-leveled dress, watches the consultation.
Standing before the prince, Nebamun presents a goblet
containing the potion the prince must take. It is indicated that the
physician's fees consisted of "slaves, cattle, copper, and natron."

Excavations of the royal archives in the capital Akhetaten
(Tell el-Amarna) founded by Amenhotep IV uncovered
correspondence with the Mitanni prince, Shama-Adda, dating
from three reigns later in the eighteenth dynasty. The prince
had requested from the king of Egypt the services of a
physician, which his own court did not have. A similar request
was made by Niqmat, king of Ugarit (the modern-day
Mediterranean port of Ras Shamra). Middle Eastern kinglets
were in the habit of turning to the Egyptian royal palace. Egypt
was known for its brilliant practitioners who, even in the Old
Kingdom, were trained at an Egyptian medical school and
passed on their knowledge from father to son. Furthermore,
certain sovereigns of neighboring countries, such as Tushratta,

Circumcision scene
Circumcision was practiced in
Egypt from the earliest times,
which was not always the case
in the Near East. Abraham
waited until he was seventy-
five before coming to Egypt
to be circumcised.
Mastaba in Giza,
Fifth dynasty

king of Mitanni, would send the statue of Ishtar to the royal
palace to help cure the king's failing health.

Clear parallels, however, have been noted between
Egyptian medical texts and their Assyrian and Babylonian
counterparts. But in terms of surprise value and humor, nothing
equals the correspondence between the king of the Hittites,
Hattusilis III, and Ramses II. Ramses's old enemy called upon
him in an attempt to secure the services of a good gynecologist,
so that his infertile sister could give birth to an heir. The
pharaoh replied: "Concerning the matter of Maranayi, my
brother's sister, I, your kindly brother, know her well. She is
sixty years old. Nobody has ever created medicine enabling to
give birth at that age. But naturally, if the Sun and the god of
storm [i.e., the two sovereigns] so wish, I will send a physician
and a good magician who can prepare her concoctions for
procreation."

To the same Hattusilis, Ramses also sent pharmacists to
provide treatment for his ophthalmia. Hattusilis also contacted
his royal friend on behalf of his vassal Kurunta, king of
Tarhuntassa, so that Ramses' physician, Paramakhu, might send
him herbs.

SPECIALIST PHYSICIANS

The renown of Egyptian physicians was such that, after the invasion of Egypt by the Persians (late sixth century BC), King Cambyses asked Wedjahorresnet, the chief physician of the pharaohs Amasis and Psamtek, to reestablish the medical school of Sais, which had had to close and was sorely missed. One upshot of the move was that the physician was accused of collaborating with the occupier. Another example of this can be found in Herodotus' reports of King Amasis sending an Egyptian eye specialist to King Cyrus. He also recounts that Darius surrounded himself with Egyptian physicians. Supported by Pliny the Elder, Herodotus also states that "Egyptian medicine is divided into specialties: each physician cares for a single illness . . . so the country is full of physicians specialized in the eyes, head, teeth, and stomach." Medical specialists would become practitioners in their own right when they had completely mastered their own domain. "In Egypt, there are physicians everywhere," concludes the early historian.

Preparation of ointment
A young girl extracting the sap from hollyhock.
Glazed terra cotta,
Palace of Ramses

Transporting the wounded
A wounded Nubian soldier is
transported from the
battlefield.
Temple of Beit el-Wali

KNOWLEDGE AND MEDICAL TREATIES

Remains of medical treatises, such as the Ebers and Edwin
Smith papyri, clearly show the Egyptians were the first to
identify the heart as "the essential organ of life." They also
said the heart was capable of "speech," in other words it
beat out a pulse. We cannot be totally sure that, after the
invention of the clepsydra, they also had the idea of
counting heartbeats using their water clock, but there are
sufficient clues to suggest as much. Much later, Herophilos,
at his native Alexandrian school, was the first Greek
physician to have used the clepsydra in his practice, in the
third century BC. It is very likely that he perfected this
process to measure his patients' pulse, a process that was
invented by a Theban physician in the seventeeth dynasty.

However, before this school of Alexandria was created,
Greek medical thinking, which had inherited close links with
Egyptian schools, had developed three main teaching
centers, at Kos, Knidos, and Croton.

"MODERN" MEDICAL PROCESSES

Before looking at these centers of research, it is worth noting
what they borrowed from the Egyptian science. The best
source of this is the head of the Kos school, Hippocrates
(450–377 BC), who, according to legend, spent three years in
Egypt. The Carlsberg papyrus reveals how, from the New
Kingdom onward, prognostics for birth were recorded, and the
ways in which physicians attempted to determine the sex of the
future child. There was the "hydromel test," or another where
the pregnant woman's urine was used to germinate different
seeds, a test that has echoes in modern theories relating to the
role of hormones, which came down to us via Byzantium.

THE INFLUENCE ON GREEK MEDICINE

When considering the legacy of Egypt and Greece in the
realms of science and medicine in general, I cannot resist
quoting the late great Egyptologist, Serge Sauneron, who died

Occupational health
The scene showers laborers
at work and accidents in the
workplace. Injuries to the arm
or eye were dealt with on-site.
Tomb painting,
Nineteenth dynasty,
Western Thebes

so unfortunately at the age of fifty: "Egypt was, in the eyes of
the Greeks, the cradle of all science and wisdom. The most
famous Hellenic scholars and philosophers crossed the sea to
seek initiation in the new sciences from priests. This voyage
was so traditional and necessary that, even if they did not make
the journey, their biographers later added the voyage to their
list of experiences anyway." There may be no reason to doubt
the visit made by Pythagoras (580–490 BC) to the pharaoh
Amasis. Or to dismiss the words of Clement of Alexandria
who, in the third century AD, wrote: "When Plato went to
Egypt, he was the all-powerful master of Athens. When in
Egypt, did he become a simple traveler and pupil?"

It is worth restating that in Egypt, cardiology, gynecology,
ophthalmology, gastroenterology, and urinology were studied
and applied with a scholarly pharmacopoeia of mineral,
animal, plant, and even human extracts. Medical papyri list
more than four hundred names of drugs and describe the many
ways of administering them: pills, decoctions, potions, syrups,
mouthwashes, macerations, plasters, poultices, eye baths,
inhalations, fumigations, enemas, swabs, vaginal irrigations, and
pessaries.

THE LEGACY OF EGYPTIAN MEDICINE: PRACTICE AND VOCABULARY

Several panaceas survived ancient Egypt and were used in European regions during medieval times. One example was the treatment of eye inflammations or headcolds with milk from a mother who has just given birth to a boy. Models of the recipient in which the milk, or colostrum, was placed are even conserved in museums. The varnished coral clay recipient was anthropomorphically shaped in the form of a crouching woman holding a naked boy. The recipe for this panacea was transmitted to the Champagne region in France where the mother of Saint Rémi of Reims was told: "Once she has given birth to a son, the happy mother's milk will cure the blind."

With their developed science and nascent humanism, the medical arts were an important feature of Egyptian civilization, and their impact was felt throughout the pharaoh's sphere of influence. Thus it was only logical that Ptolemy I, following the Persian example, set aside a considerable area in the grounds of his Mouseion in Alexandria to build a medical school, which he placed under the authority of Herophilus and Erasistratus. Alexandria, as Gustave Lefebvre states, was the gateway through which the Egyptian sciences passed into Europe, bringing with them an extraordinary breadth of medical knowledge.

A number of words used by Egyptian physicians have been passed on to us or affect us almost directly. Thus the term for a migraine comes to us from the Greek *hemicrania*, translated literally from the Egyptian *ges-tep*, meaning "half skull." Cataract is a transposition of the Egyptian *akhet-net-mu*: "collection of water." The pupil of the eye in Egyptian was called the *iret*, "image of the eye," or *hunet imyt iret*, "the girl in the eye"; the Greek word for girl was *kore*, while in Latin it was *pupilla*, and in Spanish, *une niña de los ojos*.

THE MEDICINE OF WORK

Could Greek scholars have been aware that at the start of the nineteenth dynasty, Thebes already had occupational health officers? Paintings in funerary chapels show physicians administering care to a craftsman working on a Theban necropolis who had been injured at work. Sprains, fractures, falls, eye injuries, and cuts: the specialists were on hand for everything.

IX

Architecture
and its Heritage

The impact of ancient Egypt on surrounding civilizations was huge. We only have to look at two aspects already covered, the solar calendar (the only one in early antiquity) and the origins of the alphabet, for proof of this. On both counts, humanity acknowledges the important role of Egypt. Egypt's undeniable heritage is visible in many other domains, which are not simply coincidental.

STONE ARCHITECTURE

Ancient Egyptian technical manuals on the sciences and the art of building have disappeared, but where evidence has been retrieved from the sad ruins of ancient libraries, it informs us of ancient Egyptians' very high level of knowledge, particularly in the medical sciences.

It is perhaps superfluous to talk of the splendor and originality of the country's monuments and architecture. What remains speaks for itself. However, on the question of the methods deployed by Egypt's architectural geniuses in the building of the Old Kingdom's famous pyramids, our own

FACING PAGE:
Central aisle of the hypostyle hall at Karnak
The aisle is an architectural representation of the sun reviving nature. As the sun crosses the central aisle of the great hall, the capitals of the papyriform columns resemble open buds.
Temple of Amun, Eighteenth–nineteenth dynasty, columns, Karnak

The three Great Pyramids
The Great Pyramids are the
most famous of forty or so
pyramids. They contained the
tombs of Khufu, Khafra,
and Menkaura.
Fourth dynasty, Giza

finest engineers and architects are still engaged in close
analysis of the Great Pyramid to try to find their secret.

Neither is it necessary to praise the skill and technical
sophistication required to produce sculpted masterpieces for
temples. Again, we are unable to establish just how the
sovereign's workers extracted such huge blocks of diorite or
dolerite. It is worth remembering that the king alone was
master of Egypt's many precious stone quarries. Sometimes, he
would offer blocks of stone as a gift to people he wished to
reward so that they could sculpt their own statues or stelae. But
his stone was, above all, reserved for building temples, the
houses of god, funerary chapels, and dwellings for eternity.
These stone edifices are so huge that it is as if they were created
for giants. They were designed by builders totally dependent on
their environment, and are so admirably proportioned that their
mass is difficult to evaluate. In the vast flat wastes of the desert
close to the banks of the Nile, on both sides, the Egyptians
erected vast monuments, pyramids, and pylons with pure
geometric lines. Their shapes suited the Egyptian horizon
superbly and modest copies, of later inspiration, were
unsuccessful. It took several thousand years for a daring

architect, I. M. Pei, to create a symbolic glass edifice celebrating Kheops's own burial chamber in the heart of the Louvre in Paris.

ARCHITECTURAL DECOR, A SUBJECT OF INSPIRATION

We know that architecture using clay bricks, made of Nile mud baked beneath the Egyptian sun, made an early appearance in Egyptian civilization. From the first dynasty, bricks vied with wood in the building of the most ancient religious constructions.

At the dawn of the third dynasty, King Djoser and his architect, Imhotep, brought about a veritable artistic revolution. Ancient forms were expressed in stone, right down to small gates that had previously been created with branches. The first columns supporting architraves consisted of a core of Nile mud and plants covered in papyrus. Depending whether the cover remained in place or was removed once the mark of the imprint was apparent, the proto-Doric column had a convex or concave surface. The column was copied in stone and cut into sections, a method used throughout ancient Egypt. Examples from the Old Kingdom can still be seen in front of necropolises and chapels. There are also

The quarries of Kertassi
Egypt was, and still is, a rich source of stone of all kinds, notably sandstone, granite, quartzite, and graywacke. The stone was extracted according to the approximate size desired. Everything required for the construction of monuments on Philae came from the Kertassi quarries in Nubia. Sometimes, entrepreneurs would take advantage of the environment to sculpt their own image into the rock. The also used rock engraving as their method of protest whenever a priest of Isis did not honor his contract.
Late Period

**Façade of the temple
at Luxor**
This watercolor of the temple
at Luxor was made during a
French expedition to Egypt
under Napoleon before the
edifice was excavated. We
can see the two pylons and
obelisks built by Ramses II
at the entrance. Today, the
"beautiful needle of pink
granite" on the right is
missing. It was removed by
Mehemet Ali and given to
Jean-François Champollion
and France as a gift of
gratitude to the man who
deciphered hieroglyphics and
gave Egypt back its history.
1799, Eastern Thebes

PAGE 136:
Proto-Doric columns
Proto-Doric columns
appeared in the funerary
complex of the Step Pyramid
of Djoser.
Saqqara,
Third dynasty,
Reign of Djoser

PAGE 137:
Proto-Doric colonnade
In the New Kingdom,
columns had long been
separated from walls.
The finest colonnade of
freestanding columns was
built by Queen Hatshepsut
for her mortuary temple
in Deir el-Bahri.
Chapel of Anubis,
Eighteenth dynasty,
Deir el-Bahri

**The temple
of Deir-el-Bahri**
The mortuary chapel of
Queen Hatshepsut consists of
three colonnaded terraces
with square pillars, some of
which were decorated with
the statue of the sovereign in
her mummified form. To
make the building as visible
as possible, the perimeter
wall was kept to a height
of two feet.
Temple of Hatshepsut,
Eighteenth dynasty,
Western Thebes

very elegant Middle Kingdom hypogea conserved in Beni Hasan,
which seem to be early prototypes of Doric columns, before the
latter were invented. Supreme harmony was attained in the
eighteenth dynasty. To the north of the mortuary temple of the
Queen Hatshepsut in Deir el-Bahri, the chapel of Anubis is a
beautiful example of this harmonious architectural style. Early
Greek travelers were surely impressed by the aerial rows of golden
limestone columns to which the sun brings such life, casting
shadow and light. The area might have served as an enclosure for
Phidias' masterpieces.

PAPYRIFORM COLUMNS

The most beautiful and harmonious hypostyle chamber in Egypt
is the central chamber of Ramses II's mortuary temple, the
Ramesseum. The center of the chamber is composed of an aisle
of twelve tall columns with open capitals, each representing a
single stem of papyrus and symbolizing the twelve months of the
year. To the sides are thirty-six shorter columns with closed
capitals, suggesting the thirty-six decans of the calendar.

VUE PERSPECTIVE DE LA GRANDE SALLE HYPOSTYLE DU TEMPLE DE KARNAK

This same symbolism of the months of the year can also be found in our basilicas and cathedrals. One great example is that of the Justinian foundation on Mount Sinai, devoted to Saint Catherine, where each of the central columns is inscribed with the name of the corresponding month.

THE IONIC CAPITAL

It appears almost certain that the elegant Egyptian capitals decorated with reliefs of Egyptian lilies influenced the shape of the Ionic capital, with its characteristic volutes.

OVOLI

Bunches of grapes, symbolizing the blood of god, the divine harvest, were a feature of ceiling borders in Osirian royal canopies of the nineteenth dynasty. The Greeks seem to have borrowed the motif, transforming it into ovoli for decorative bands. A connection could also be made here with such motifs as *tori* and cornices.

Cross-section of a hypostyle chamber
The similarity between this ground plan and that of a Western basilica is clear. The best prototype of a hypostyle hall can be found at the Ramesseum, Ramses II's mortuary chamber.
Nineteenth reconstruction by Georges Perrot and Charles Chipiez

FACING PAGE:
Proto-Ionic pillar
The Ethiopian flower
influenced Ionic capitals
throughout Egypt.
Karnak

Closed papyrus capitals
The multistem column
represents bundled plant
stems and has a capital in the
form of a closed bud.
Eighteenth dynasty,
Temple at Luxor

Osiride pillar
The entrance courtyards at
the Ramesseum were flanked
by Osiride pillars, adorned
with a statue of the king, his
body swathed in a shroud.
These statues were added to
the pillars and were not
structural supports.
In Greek architecture, on the
other hand, architraves were
supported by the heads of
atlantes.
Ramesseum,
Nineteenth dynasty,
Western Thebes

Royal pavilion

The New Empire saw the use of three successive canopies, one inside the other, with highly symbolic capitals. The decoration on the first ceiling resembles grapes. The sovereigns here present are King Amenophis III and Queen Tiy.

Drawing after polychrome relief, Eighteenth dynasty, Western Thebes

FACING PAGE:

Osiride canopies

In later periods, Osiride canopies became composite and were no longer superposed. The capitals decorating this Osiride pavilion, however, were stacked.

Tomb painting, Nineteenth dynasty, Western Thebes

"Tomb of Vines"
Sennefer cut a tomb out of the
Theban mountain. In the
burial chamber, the ceiling
has been painted with a grape
vine "supported" by square
pillars.
Tomb of Sennefer,
Eighteenth dynasty,
Western Thebes

ARBORS OF VINES

The ovoli of Greek architectural decoration were
originally represented as bunches of grapes in Egyptian
architecture, which was fond of using the vine's fruit and
wide leaves to depict real decorative garden arbors. The
vine and grapes, swollen with the blood of Osiris, also
announced the arrival of the flood, the New Year, and the
return of the deceased. A Theban lord by the name of
Sennefer, the minister of agriculture under Amenhotep II,
used such scenery to transform his own burial chamber,
hollowed out of the mountains, into the most sumptuous
of bowers. The powerful symbolism of the vine was never
forgotten by Egyptians who, in the Coptic Christian age,
used them to decorate the friezes of their churches (see the
frieze of the church of Bawit in the Louvre). The grape
motif is also to be found on the capitals and columns of
churches in the West.

SKY AND TEMPLE FLOOR

Temples were designed to depict the universe produced by the Creator. The ceilings of the holy of holies, and also of certain galleries, were often decorated with five-pointed stars. The stone paving trod by bare feet was uneven and may, to the uninformed observer keen on straight lines and smooth surfaces, look like the result of poor workmanship. This *opus incertum* later inspired the Romans and the whole of Europe, and was actually deliberate. The effect was intended to represent the cracked thirsty surface of the Black Earth before the arrival of the salutary flood: yet one more of ancient Egypt's heritages.

EGYPTIAN FRIEZES

The metopes and triglyphs that decorated the entablature of Grecian temples with narrative friezes were probably inspired

Chapel of the goddess Hathor
On the terrace of the temple of Dendera, a chapel was built to receive the goddess at New Year. The capitals of the small columns are decorated on each side with a human face with the ears of the divine cow. In the Middle and New Kingdoms, only one side of the capital featured this decoration.
Temple at Dendera,
Roman era

Ruins of the Buhen fortress
View of the whole fortress
when it was discovered.
Buhen, Middle Kingdom,
Twelth dynasty,
Nubia, second cataract
(near the Sudanese border)

FACING PAGE:
Buhen, reconstruction
The extensive ruins, buried
beneath the sand, enabled the
great archaeologist and
architect Walter Emery to
create a perfect reconstruction
of the fortress. The illustartion
shows the barbican, including
two fortified sections and
a drawbridge.

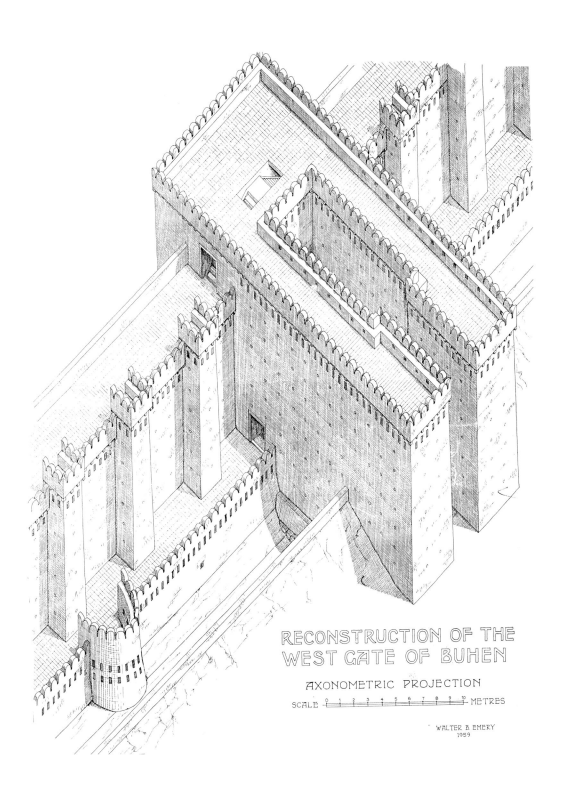

RECONSTRUCTION OF THE
WEST GATE OF BUHEN

AXONOMETRIC PROJECTION

SCALE 0 1 2 3 4 5 6 7 8 9 10 METRES

WALTER B. EMERY
1959

The Krak des Chevaliers
The Crusaders were undoubtedly inspired by the elegant architecture and advanced defense system of the citadel of Kadesh and attempted to create copies in situ.
c. 1180,
Syria

by the horizontal ornamental friezes beneath the cornices of small Osirian chapels in the nineteenth dynasty. These were made up of a series of decorative rectangles and vertical bars. The Greeks used their own friezes, metopes, and triglyphs to depict tableaux of sculpted mythological subjects.

ROYAL AND CIVIL ARCHITECTURE

Only stone extracted from its original quarry was permitted to shelter the divine. Of palaces and houses built of baked clay, only traces of their foundations remain. As discussed above, Egyptian bricks were as perishable as humankind, although some have survived to the present day.

MILITARY ARCHITECTURE

Our heritage from ancient Egypt is vast, and its routes of transmission are multiple and sometimes quite surprising. Let us take the example of military architecture and the way fortified castles were designed. The appearance of castles dates back to the Old Kingdom at least, but their ruins are less well conserved than post Middle Kingdom examples, a period when circumstances forced the country's rulers to protect their frontiers against the first invaders from the East. Egyptians also had to resist invasion from Cush, today's Sudan, whose hunger for Egyptian gold drove them over the Nubian borders.

In the Middle Kingdom, the "Walls of the Prince," to the east of the Delta, was made up of a succession of small forts that were not actually connected. Unfortunately, little remains of these forts. Despite their desire to encourage trade with southern-most regions, the sovereigns Sesostris and Amenemhat were also forced to defend themselves against pillagers and raiders from beyond Egypt, to the south of the Nile's second cataract. Remains of what are extremely impressive buildings, commanded by Sesostris III and covering ten miles to the south of the second cataract, still survive.

The citadel of Buhen (Wadi Halfa) was impressive in its size, occupying a vast surface of twenty-six acres. The clay brick walls were sixteen feet thick and thirty-six feet high. When Nubia was threatened by engulfment from the waters of the Aswan High Dam, the Sadd el-Aali, the emergency work carried out on the citadel gave the architect Walter Emery a chance to clear the sand from its impressive ruins. The walls of the Buhen fortress were dominated by protruding square crenellated towers. At the base, a rampart, paved in bricks and protected by a parapet, overlooked a moat of more than twenty-six feet wide and twenty-one feet deep. The counterscarp was crowned with a narrow brick-covered patrol path. Circular turrets were fitted with loopholes, directed to launch arrows in three directions. Its extraordinary majestic fortified gate to the west was built into a barbican, inside which two further sections, reinforced by a drawbridge, afforded almost total security. These brick ruins have now disappeared beneath the water of Lake Nasser.

During the New Kingdom, from the reign of the great Thutmose III, the Egyptian presence in Middle Eastern cities and regions helped reinforce their military defenses, greatly contributing to the upkeep of order in these regions. The land of Canaan, for example, was equipped with pharaoh-built strongholds. If control over them was ever lost in battle, their new occupiers would maintain them for long periods afterwards over the centuries. Much later when the first Crusaders arrived in the region, the West discovered the Egyptian fortifications for the first time, which were clearly more elaborate than their own primitive versions. Defensive architecture had been developed for centuries in Egypt, and Crusaders even copied it in situ, before they went on to export it. The well-known Krak des Chevaliers is the most spectacular demonstration of this.

An episode from the battle of Kadesh
Ramses II's army besieged the citadel of Kadesh, on the Orontes River, to wrest control of the citadel from the Hittite king and his allies.
Relief from the Great Temple of Abu Simbel,
Nineteenth dynasty,
Nubia

X

Words that Traveled

With its solid civilized foundations, early Egypt was very attractive to its closest eastern neighbors in Palestine and Canaan, and later the Hebrews, who were most influenced by the country. Naturally, Greeks and Romans were also drawn to the country and its appeal lasted thousands of years, for many different reasons.

It is only natural that animals and plants native to Africa retained their original name. Thus the words *geseh, benu, heby,* and *beneret* still exist for the gazelle, palm tree, ibis, and date palm. The same transfer took place for materials: *hebeny,* or ebony, in Hebrew *habnim* and *ebenos* in Greek; *neter(y)* for niter and natron; or the word "gum" that comes from *kemyt,* or *komi* in Coptic, *kommi* in Greek, *Gummi* in German, and *gomme* in French. There are also geographic terms such as *wh't,* oasis. Sometimes the name of a technique has also been passed on, such as *kemi,* chemistry or "black" magic, which probably gave Egypt its name: *kemet.* In Arabic, *al-kemi* means alchemy, "the science of the Black Land."

The phoenix
The legendary blue bird that arose from the ashes to visit Egypt for many centuries was represented on a wall of Queen Nefertari's burial chamber. The name "phoenix" comes from a distortion of the Egyptian word *benu.*
Tomb of Nefertari,
Nineteenth dynasty,
Valley of the Queens,
Western Thebes

PAGE 152:
Statue of an ibis
In its native ancient Egypt, the ibis was called *heb.* These days, this species can be found only in Ethiopia and zoos around the world.
Bronze and painted
stuccoed wood,
Saite Period,
Musée du Louvre, Paris

Workers carrying sacks
The scribe is seated at the top
recording the number of
sacks. The contents of the
sacks are being emptied into
the opening. The word "sack"
has remained practically
unchanged for thousands
of years.
Model of a granary,
Middle Kingdom,
Musée du Louvre, Paris

In the flower world, Egypt's two most important flowers
have left their mark. The blue lotus was given the name *sechem*.
Hebrew picked it up to create the name Shechama (Suzanne),
the wife of the Judean King Susinna, which led to a town in
Iran being called Shushan, today called Susa. Next to the
sensuous blue lotus grew the *nefer*, a beautiful white flower with
bountiful petals; its name means "beautiful," "radiant," "full of
vitality." In the feminine, the proper name Neferet appeared,
even before the pyramids were built, as a name for charming
young girls whose beauty was predestined. During the Arab
occupation of Egypt, the word *nefer* became *el-nefer*, which
became *nénuphar* in French.

In a similar vein, the flower, pronounced "hai-rai-rai", is
also to be found, following the classical phonetic law, in the
word "lily."

We do not have to delve far into the Bible to encounter the
grandson of Aaron, by the name of Phinehas. The name
descended directly through the rules of Nile onomastics, where
the name Pa-Nehesy, common under the New Kingdom, was
given to people from the south with "copper" skin. Another

proper name, adopted in the Bible, is that of the husband of the woman of disrepute, Potiphar, a name drawn from the Egyptian *pa-di-pa-Ra*, meaning "given by the god Ra." Then there is the name of Moses that comes directly from the word *mose*, "he who is born," an abbreviation in Egypt used in theophoric names, such as Ramose, Ptahmose or Ptahmes, Thutmose, and Ramessesu.

Finally, among the common words passed on from the venerable language of the pharaohs (a word meaning "great house" or "palace" in ancient Egypt), we will also cite vocabulary related to the Egyptian word *sek*, "to collect." Via the Hebrew, Greek (*sakkos*), and Latin (*saccus*), it came to designate a fairly everyday object: the sack. Among all these different categories of words, let us not forget the transmission of more professional vocabulary, passed on with the techniques themselves.

A royal favorite, the princess of el-Bersheh
Young girl parading with blue lotuses.
Girls of the court were called *sechen* (or lotuses) to identify their standing. *Sechen* later became the name Suzanne.
Middle Kingdom,
Egyptian Museum, Cairo

A MUCH TRAVELED EGYPTIAN WORD

One word that has journeyed extensively to reach us from the banks of the Nile is the term "adobe." It appeared in France at the end of the nineteenth century to designate a sun-dried clay brick used in construction. The brick was the essential ingredient of Egyptian civil architecture for more than four thousand years. It was made from the mud which was, up until the construction of the Aswan High Dam, deposited by the floods every year. Nothing could be easier to fashion than this brick. Its creation was free of constraints and major inconveniences of any kind.

The brick was created by mixing mud deposited from the banks of the Ethiopian Atbara during the annual flood of the Nile with burned straw and water. After several days' fermentation and kneading of the mixture, a substance called *muna* was obtained, a name that has survived into modern Egyptian. This mixture was then poured in rectangular wooden molds, allowed to half-dry, then removed and dried completely in the sun. For thousands of years, century after century, this brick was used to construct royal palaces, and

Rectangular brick mold
with wooden handle.
Sketch by G. Goyon

FACING PAGE:
Manufacture of bricks
Egyptian and Semite
workers at work
Tomb of Rekhmara,
Eighteenth dynasty, Thebes

Manufacturing bricks
Drawing after Champollion
Theban tomb of Rekhmara

humble *fellah* abodes alike. Natural stone, as we have seen, was reserved for the construction of divine buildings.

On one of the walls of the Theban funerary chapel of Rekhmara, a vizier to Thutmose III, we can see illustrations of beardless Egyptians and Semite workers (not slaves), identifiable by their small pointed beards (see pages 160 and 174). Egyptians and Semites were depicted simply making bricks and building walls with them. Building work was never deemed a degrading occupation, reserved for subordinates or slaves, and clay bricks have always been made all over Egypt. Even during excavations, when repairs or reinforcements were required, we would create the same time-honored brick belonging to the land of the Nile.

When, after the Hegira (AD 622), the Arabs settled in Egypt, the old name for the brick, *djeba*, formally the *djebet* of Ramesside times, lost some of its tonality and became the *tobe* of Christian Egypt, as Coptic Egypt adopted Greek letters to write its language.

The word passed into Arabic in the form *toba*. Throughout the Arab conquest of North Africa, *toba* became the ideal material for the construction of houses in Tunisia, Morocco, and Algeria. The Arab conquerors moved onto Spain, where they also initiated inhabitants into the use of the clay brick. In Spain, the article *el* (the) was placed before the word *tobe*, or *toba*, which became *el-toba*, then adobe.

When Spain, in turn, undertook its conquest of Mexico, the adobe went with it and quickly became a popular building material. The name traveled with the brick to Mexico.

The word was then transported to the United States and the Spanish connection might have led some to believe that it was imported into France in the nineteenth century by transatlantic travelers. The reality behind its final journey is much more amusing, and it appears that soldiers of the imperial army of Napoleon III brought back the adobe with them as a prize after their disastrous Mexican adventure.

Manufacturing bricks
As the practice of making bricks traveled accross the globe, so did the language associated with it.

XI

The Legacy
of Egypt in Israel,
or Joseph and Egypt

From the Old Kingdom onward, Egypt entertained generally peaceful relations with its immediate neighbors, the Bedouins, who lived near the borders on the eastern banks of the Mediterranean. Egyptian presence even reached beyond Byblos, shown by the remains of Egyptian sanctuaries, and extended through the regions of Canaan, Syria, and Palestine, as their contacts with the miners of Sinai demonstrated. Inhabitants of these regions could request peaceful entry into Egypt at the military border posts, as depicted in the famous tomb painting of Beni Hasan.

This tomb painting illustrating the funerary chapels of a Middle Egyptian governor is a typical allusion to the era of the biblical Patriarchs (see Genesis 12:10, for example). In it, we witness the arrival at the edge of the Red Sea of the thirty-seven Semites, led by their chief, an Asian by the name of Abshai. They are represented in national costume accompanied by their wives and children, playing the lyre, with a donkey out in front. The purpose of their journey is to meet the Egyptians and sell them galena for the production of antimony, required to protect the King of Egypt's eyes.

FACING PAGE:
Ramses II in mourning
This artist's study shows the face of Ramses II with a stubbled chin. It was the practice to grow a beard as a sign of mourning, a custom still followed by Jews today.
Theban painting,
Nineteenth dynasty,
Western Thebes

**The arrival
of the Semites in Egypt**
The text states that the group
was composed of thirty-seven
people—men, women, and
children—who were
introduced to the royal scribe
Neferhotep. The men carried
lyres, bows, and sticks. Not far
from them is a group of
elegant women wearing small
boots to protect their feet
from the sand.
Tomb painting,
Middle Kingdom, Beni Hasan,
Twelfth dynasty

The Semite group is described as made up of *hekau
khasut*, or "heads of foreign countries," a term that
sometimes described invaders. Later they infiltrated Egypt at
the end of the Middle Kingdom, and were known by the
Greek name of Hyksos. We have already seen how the
Bedouin workers in the Sinai received their first lessons in
reading, writing, and "comparative translation" in the
company of Egyptian scribes during their expeditions to
turquoise mines. In the same way, Semites, returning from
Egypt, came to naturally adopt Egyptian words in their own
language, like *neteri* for "natron," or *ideni*, which became
etum, or "red linen."

The exchange also worked in the other direction,
with the ancient Egyptians adopting everyday objects from
their close neighbors, such as the lyre. The lyre is also
depicted being carried by Egyptian musicians from the early
New Kingdom in the painting at Beni Hasan. The harp,
meanwhile, a perfect instrument for sedentary peoples, also
appeared in depictions of concerts in very early Old
Kingdom Egypt. The harp was played sitting on the
ground, almost horizontally. Over time, the instrument
grew in volume and elegance before becoming, in the New
Kingdom, the instrument that it is today, its magnificent
resonating body embraced in the arms of the musician and
played in the vertical position. It is in this form
that it reached the modern West, with some alterations
to detail.

After the Hyksos's departure from Egyptian soil,
the Egyptians also benefited from another valuable
contribution from their Asian occupiers, namely the use
of the horse and cart with double harness. The Semite
occupiers, for their part, left Egypt with new customs and
new expressions for their language. Thus, they came to
adopt the practice of circumcision, already undertaken
by Old Kingdom Egyptians. They also inherited the
wonders of Egyptian medicine which, as Herodotus
recalled, was practiced by physicians with "broad and
deep knowledge."

The same proper names started to appear in both ethnic
groups. Semites born in Egypt, the land of Kemi, the Black
Earth, were given slightly adapted Egyptian names by their
parents. Merari or Meru were drawn from the word *mery*,
"love." Pachehor came from the *pa-ché-Hor*, or "portion of
Horus." There were also combined names, such as Putial,
from the Egyptian *pa-di-El*, or "given by the god El." I
have already refered to the name Phinehas, from the
Egyptian *pa-nehesy*, "the dark skinned man," or biblical
names such as Sushana, which gave Suzanne, and comes
from the Egyptian word *sechen*, meaning water-lily. Let us
not forget the name of the husband of the fickle wife of the
pharaoh's "eunuch," Potiphar, created from *pa-di-pa-Râ*,
"given by Ra." There is also the name of Joseph's wife,
Asenath, made up of *n (y)-s (y)-Neith*, "belonging to the
goddess Neith."

Royal harps
Images of the most beautiful
Egyptian harps decorated one
of the walls of Ramses III's
burial chamber. Such harps
were played standing up.
Tomb of Ramses III,
Twentieth dynasty, Valley
of the Kings, Western Thebes

FACING PAGE:
Classic harp
The harp was a typically
Egyptian musical instrument.
In the Old Kingdom, the harp
was a small, boat-shaped
instrument played seated on
the ground. During the New
Kingdom, harps became larger
and were played standing up.
Wood, leather, strings (modern),
Eighteenth dynasty,
Musée du Louvre, Paris

In Egypt, a sage was said to have lived to the age of one
hundred and ten. This is the age the Bible accords Joseph
and Joshua.

The customs of mourning did not escape the Semites'
attention either. So when someone died, the men of the
family let their beard grow a set number of days, a custom
respected today by some Jews. Mourners would cover their
heads in dust and employ professional mourners to show
their affliction. Men would adopt the same posture, curled
up on themselves, "their head on their knees": *djadja* or *tep-
her-maset.*

In Egypt, anointment was an important ceremonial
feature. Pharaoh, the first, was anointed at his coronation.
The Hittite princess was also anointed, a privilege conferred by
Ramses himself through his ambassador when they were
married. The sovereign would also issue royal anointment for his
high officials, or acknowledge a royal member from a foreign
vessel arriving in Egypt by pouring lotus oil on his or her head.

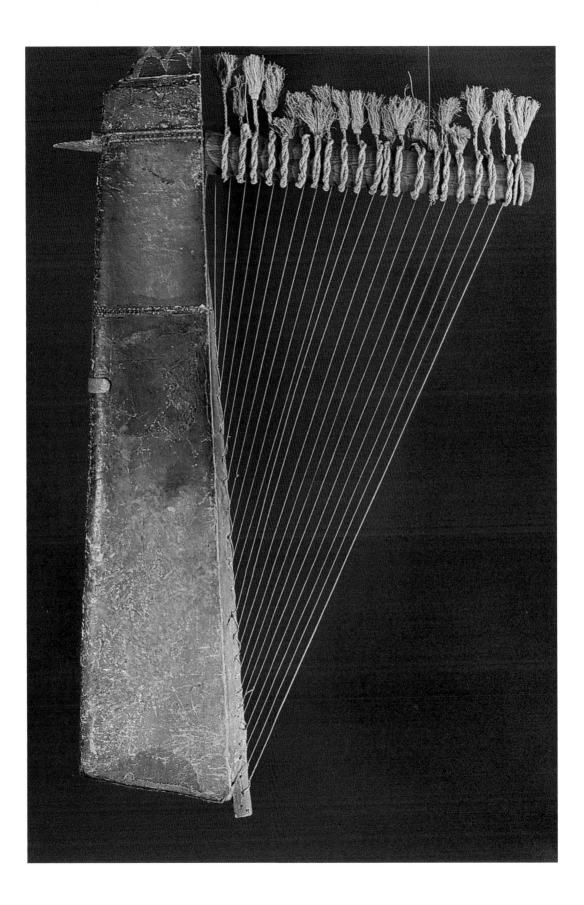

Anointment was a practice also adopted by the Hebrews, who gave it a specific meaning. Unction was reserved for the king alone who, on reception, would became the vassal of Yahweh.

In biblical writings there are expressions borrowed from the Egyptians that inspired their Semite neighbors. So Yahweh promised to make Jeremiah (15:20) "a fortified wall of bronze." However, the earlier Egyptian expression for an insurmountable rampart, embodied in Pharaoh, was "the bronze wall" in Egyptian, or *sebty n bia en pet*, "the wall of the miracle from the sky," meteorite iron.

These final allusions to the holy writings of the Bible should encourage us to ask more questions concerning the relationship between the Egyptians and their eastern neighbors, the Semites. We have found humble Egyptian inscriptions, almost incantations, to defend themselves against potentially hostile Semite masses. In them, they mention the cities of Sechem, Ascalon, and above all Jerusalem, which we learn already existed in the 13th dynasty. The legendary foundation of these cities by David happened in the Bible in a much earlier period.

Mourners on a boat
Professional mourners—usually women—were the most visible sign of affliction following a death. They were present at the home of the deceased, in the funerary procession, and at the entrance to the tomb. They would wail and sing praises to the dead, and cover their heads with dust. This custom was adopted by the Hebrews after they left Egypt. This scene shows the last stretch of the Nile before reaching the tomb.
Tomb painting, Eighteenth-nineteenth dynasty, Western Thebes

FACING PAGE:
Farewell to the dead
The moment when mourning reached its loudest volume was when the mummy was stood before the tomb.
Tomb painting, Nineteenth dynasty, Western Thebes

Masons at work

Proof that legends are not always true. This scene shows total equality between Semite workers, with their short pointed beards and lighter skin, and beardless fellahs with their darker skin. The Semites show no signs of servitude.

Rekhmara, after Champollion

Another important question concerns the relationship of the Hebrews to the Egyptians. Among the archaeological remains we have, there is no evidence suggesting the Hebrews, supposedly a suffering race, servile to the Egyptians and ill-treated, were forced to create clay bricks for the pharaoh in desert areas far from the Nile.

As I have stated elsewhere, the reality was very different. A painting decorating the funerary chapel of Rekhmara, vizier of Thutmose III, even reproduces an instructive scene where Semites and Egyptians are depicted making bricks, working and cooperating together freely, side by side. They are also shown working together in the creation of a wall.

In the nineteenth dynasty that followed, that of Ramses, the Bedouins, Egypt's neighbors, often crossed the border, called the Walls of the Prince, in the hope of gaining employment on the pharaoh's building sites for set periods. Their role consisted of transporting vast blocks of stone to construct temples in the king's northern capital. Naturally, I am not alluding here to the many Canaanites, Egyptianized Semites entrusted with important functions for pharaoh's palace.

Excavations in Egypt, and recently in Israel, by the Israeli archaeologists Israel Finkelstein and Neil Asher Silbermann have confirmed that biblical texts were written long after the events they describe and were based on imaginative themes more intended to encourage the birth of

a nation. In the quest to find out what Egypt did pass on to the people of Israel, we must also ask questions of the Bible's description of Joseph, son of the Israeli Jacob, and his miraculous adventure; there are questions here too concerning the legendary activities of Moses. After the publication of the Holy Bible, and before the deciphering of hieroglyphics by Jean-François Champollion (1822), we had no other text in our possession to describe ancient Egypt. We did not even know any actual names of the "pharaohs," the title given to Egypt's sovereigns, first taught to us by the Bible. The best way to ask these questions is to refer directly to the text of the Pentateuch.

Detail from the previous illustration
Semitic worker
Tomb of the vizier Rekhmara,
Eighteenth dynasty,
Western Thebes

ABRAHAM IN EGYPT, GENESIS 12:1

Abraham's original name, Abram, was changed after
circumcision. His wife Sarai became Sarah, here is the text:

*Yahweh said to Abram, "Leave your country, your
kindred . . . for a country which I shall show you. . . . So
Abram went as Yahweh told him . . . Abram was seventy-
five years old when he left Haran. Abram took his wife
Sarai . . . all the possessions they had amassed and the
people they had acquired in Haran. They set off for the
land of Canaan, and arrived there. . . . Then Abram made
his way stage by stage to the Negeb.*

GENESIS 12:10

*There was a famine in the country, and Abram went down to
Egypt to stay there for a time, since the famine in the country
was severe. When he was about to enter Egypt, he said to his
wife Sarai, "Look, I know you are a beautiful woman. When
the Egyptians see you they will say, 'That is his wife,' and
they will kill me but leave you alive. Therefore please tell
them you are my sister, so that they may treat me well because
of you and spare my life out of regard for you." When Abram
arrived in Egypt the Egyptians did indeed see that the woman
was very beautiful. When Pharaoh's officials saw her they
sang her praises to Pharaoh and the woman was taken into
Pharaoh's household. And Abram was very well treated
because of her and received flocks, oxen, donkeys, men and
women slaves, she-donkeys and camels. But Yahweh inflicted
severe plagues on Pharaoh and his household because of
Abram's wife Sarai. So Pharaoh summoned Abram and said,
"What is this you have done to me? Why did you not tell me
she was your wife? Why did you say, 'She is my sister,' so
that I took her to be my wife? Now, here is your wife. Take
her and go!" And Pharaoh gave his people orders about him;
they sent him on his way with his wife and all his
possessions.*

This story shows the appeal of Egypt to its immediate
neighbors, the Bedouins, whose own habitat, the Canaan
desert, was hostile in climate and environment. When they

first arrived in the land of Pharaoh, Bedouins and their behavior may have appeared peculiar to Egyptians, whose lifestyles and civilization were gentle, sedentary, and tinged with humanism. We have a glimpse here of the attitude held by these guardians of "flocks, oxen, and donkeys" toward the wealthier Egyptian lifestyle. Here the patriarch Abraham cynically accepts their wealthier lifestyle, due to the privileged position Pharaoh accords his wife. However, Yahweh was watching over his children and their wayward behavior. Now let us follow what else Yahweh masterminded on the banks of the Nile.

JOSEPH AND HIS BROTHERS, GENESIS 37:1

This is the account of Jacob and his descendants. Joseph was a seventeen-year-old young man. He took care of the flocks with the sons of Bilhah and Zilpah, his father's wives. Joseph told his father about the bad things his brothers were doing. Israel loved Joseph more than all his sons because Joseph had been born in Israel's old age. So he made Joseph a special robe with long sleeves.

Joseph's brothers saw that their father loved him more than any of them. They hated Joseph and couldn't speak to him on friendly terms. Joseph had a dream and when he told his brothers, they hated him even more. He said to them, "Please listen to the dream I had. We were tying grain into bundles out in the field, and suddenly mine stood up. It remained standing while your bundles gathered around my bundle and bowed down to it." Then his brothers asked him, "Are you going to be our King or rule us?" They hated him even more for his dreams and his words. Then he had another dream, and he told it to his brothers. "Listen," he said, "I had another dream: I saw the sun, the moon, and 11 stars bowing down to me."

When he told his father and his brothers, his father criticized him by asking, "What's this dream you had? Will your mother and I and your brothers come and bow down in front of you?" So his brothers were jealous of him, but his father kept thinking about these things.

JOSEPH SOLD BY HIS BROTHERS, GENESIS, 37:12

His brothers had gone to take care of their father's flocks at Shechem. Israel then said to Joseph, "Your brothers are taking care of the flocks at Shechem. I'm going to send you to them." Joseph responded, "I'll go." So Israel said, "See how your brothers and the flocks are doing, and bring some news back to me." Then he sent Joseph away from the Hebron Valley. When Joseph came to Shechem, a man found him wandering around in the open country. "What are you looking for?" the man asked. Joseph replied, "I'm looking for my brothers. Please tell me where they're taking care of their flocks." The man said, "They moved on from here. I heard them say, 'Let's go to Dothan.'" So Joseph went after his brothers and found them at Dothan.

GENESIS 37:18

They saw him from a distance. Before he reached them, they plotted to kill him. They said to each other, "Look, here comes that master dreamer! Let's kill him, throw him into one of the cisterns, and say that a wild animal has eaten him. Then we'll see what happens to his dreams."

When Reuben heard this, he tried to save Joseph from their plot. "Let's not kill him," he said. "Let's not have any bloodshed. Put him into that cistern that's out in the desert, but don't hurt him." Reuben wanted to rescue Joseph from them and bring him back to his father. So when Joseph reached his brothers, they stripped him of his special robe with long sleeves. Then they took him and put him into an empty cistern. It had no water in it. As they sat down to eat, they saw a caravan of Ishmaelites coming from Gilead. Their camels were carrying the materials for cosmetics, medicine, and embalming. They were on their way to take them to Egypt. Judah asked his brothers, "What will we gain by killing our brother and covering up his death? Let's sell him to the Ishmaelites. Let's not hurt him, because he is our brother, our own flesh and blood." His brothers agreed. As the Midianite merchants were passing by, the brothers pulled Joseph out of the cistern. They sold him to the Ishmaelites for twenty shekels.

The Ishmaelites took him to Egypt. When Reuben came back to the cistern and saw that Joseph was no longer there, he tore his clothes in grief. He went back to his brothers and said, "The boy isn't there! What am I going to do?" So they took Joseph's robe, killed a goat, and dipped the robe in the blood. Then they brought the special robe with long sleeves to their father and said, "We found this. You better examine it to see whether it's your son's robe or not." He recognized it and said, "It is my son's robe! A wild animal has eaten him! Joseph must have been torn to pieces!" Then, to show his grief, Jacob tore his clothes, put sackcloth around his waist, and mourned for his son a long time. All his other sons and daughters came to comfort him, but he refused to be comforted. He said, "No, I will mourn for my son until I die." This is how Joseph's father cried over him.

JOSEPH'S EARLY DAYS IN EGYPT, GENESIS 39:1

Joseph had been taken to Egypt. Potiphar, one of Pharaoh's Egyptian officials and captain of the guard, bought him from the Ishmaelites who had taken him there. Yahweh was with Joseph, so he became a successful man. He worked in the house of his Egyptian master.

Joseph's master saw that Yahweh was with him and that Yahweh made everything he did successful. Potiphar liked Joseph so much that he made him his trusted servant. He put him in charge of his household and everything he owned. From that time on Yahweh blessed the Egyptian's household because of Joseph. Therefore, Yahweh's blessing was on everything Potiphar owned in his house and in his fields. So he left all that he owned in Joseph's care. He wasn't concerned about anything except the food he ate.

The story evokes the Egyptian atmosphere well, particularly with the well-placed use of the name Potiphar which, as we have seen, is formed from the Egyptian *pa-di-pa-ra*, or "given by the god Ra." Potiphar was invested with an important mission at the palace, probably working for the royal ladies; eunuchs, however, did not exist in Egypt. The writer of the text was probably influenced by the palace of Jerusalem or court of Iran.

The name Pharaoh was, as already stated, revealed by the Bible, long before Champollion deciphered Egyptian hieroglyphics in the early nineteenth century. The name is composed of two words *per-aa*, meaning "great house," transformed by the Greek into *pher-ao*, which became "pharaoh." The term was used at the start of the New Kingdom to refer to the palace during the dual reign of Hatshepsut and her nephew Thutmose III. It was then used by extension to designate the sovereign and the "great house," in the same way as we refer to the White House or Kremlin.

JOSEPH AND THE SEDUCTRESS,
GENESIS 39:7–20

After a while his master's wife began to desire Joseph, so she said, "Come to bed with me." But Joseph refused and said to her, "My master doesn't concern himself with anything in the house. He trusts me with everything he owns. No one in this house is greater than I. He's kept nothing back from me except you, because you're his wife. How could I do such a wicked thing and sin against God?" Although she kept asking Joseph day after day, he refused to go to bed with her or be with her.

One day he went into the house to do his work, and none of the household servants were there. She grabbed him by his clothes and said, "Come to bed with me!" But he ran outside and left his clothes in her hand. When she realized that he had gone but had left his clothes behind, she called her household servants and said to them, "Look! My husband brought this Hebrew here to fool around with us. He came in and tried to go to bed with me, but I screamed as loud as I could. As soon as he heard me scream, he ran outside and left his clothes with me." She kept Joseph's clothes with her until his master came home. Then she told him the same story: "The Hebrew slave you brought here came in and tried to fool around with me. But when I screamed, he ran outside and left his clothes with me."

When Potiphar heard his wife's story, especially when she said, "This is what your slave did to me," he became very angry. So Joseph's master arrested him and put him in the same prison where the king's prisoners were kept.

With the intervention of the wife of Potiphar we arrive at the heart of the story. It is apparent that the writer was directly inspired by one of the liveliest passages of the "Tale of Two Brothers," the Orbiney papyrus, conserved at the British Museum. The tale is an account of some of the stormiest events of the Ramesside era and was popular in the nineteenth dynasty. The hero, who is working for his older brother, is provoked by this older brother's wife in a similar situation. However, rather than be incarcerated like Joseph, the hero flees and encounters strange, unexpected, and wonderful adventures.

According to the text in the Bible, Joseph was probably put under house arrest in the citadel of Tjaru (Sile), at the eastern tip of the Delta, the first point of the important border post, not far from Avaris, the capital of the Hyksos invaders. Later on Pi-Ramses, Ramses II's capital, was built there.

JOSEPH IN PRISON,
GENESIS 39:20

> *While Joseph was in prison, Yahweh was with him.*
> *Yahweh reached out to him with his unchanging love and*
> *gave him protection. Yahweh also put Joseph on good terms*
> *with the warden. So the warden placed Joseph in charge of*
> *all the prisoners who were in that prison. Joseph became*
> *responsible for everything that they were doing. The*
> *warden paid no attention to anything under Joseph's care*
> *because Yahweh was with Joseph and made whatever he*
> *did successful.*

JOSEPH INTERPRETS PHARAOH'S OFFICERS'
DREAMS, GENESIS 40:1–23

> *Later the king's cupbearer and his baker offended their*
> *master, the king of Egypt. Pharaoh was angry with his*
> *chief cupbearer and his chief baker. He put them in the*
> *prison of the captain of the guard, the same place where*
> *Joseph was a prisoner. The captain of the guard assigned*
> *them to Joseph, and he took care of them.*
> *After they had been confined for some time, both*
> *prisoners—the cupbearer and the baker for the king of*

Egypt—had dreams one night. Each man had a dream with its own special meaning. When Joseph came to them in the morning, he saw that they were upset. So he asked these officials of Pharaoh who were with him in his master's prison, "Why do you look so unhappy today?" "We both had dreams," they answered him, "but there's no one to tell us what they mean." "Isn't God the only one who can tell what they mean?" Joseph asked them. "Why don't you tell me all about them."

So the chief cupbearer told Joseph his dream. He said: "In my dream a grapevine with three branches appeared in front of me. Soon after it sprouted it blossomed. Then its clusters ripened into grapes. Pharaoh's cup was in my hand, so I took the grapes and squeezed them into it. I put the cup in Pharaoh's hand." "This is what it means," Joseph said to him. "The three branches are three days. In the next three days Pharaoh will release you and restore you to your position. You will put Pharaoh's cup in his hand as you used to do when you were his cupbearer. Remember me when things go well for you, and please do me a favor. Mention me to Pharaoh, and get me out of this prison. I was kidnapped from the land of the Hebrews, and even here I've done nothing to deserve being put in this prison."

The chief baker saw that the meaning Joseph had given to the cupbearer's dream was good. So he said to Joseph, "I had a dream too. In my dream three baskets of white baked goods were on my head. The top basket contained all kinds of baked goods for Pharaoh, but the birds were eating them out of the basket on my head." "This is what it means," Joseph replied. "The three baskets are three days. In the next three days Pharaoh will cut off your head and hang your dead body on a pole. The birds will eat the flesh from your bones."

Two days later, on his birthday, Pharaoh had a special dinner prepared for all his servants. Of all his servants he gave special attention to the chief cupbearer and the chief baker. He restored the chief cupbearer to his position. So the cupbearer put the cup in Pharaoh's hand. But he hung the chief baker just as Joseph had said in his interpretation. Nevertheless, the chief cupbearer didn't remember Joseph. He forgot all about him.

It is surprising that a young man, more used to looking after his father's flocks than reading dreams, could so easily interpret the dreams of his noble jail companions. But as he himself declares, "Isn't God the only one who can tell what they mean?" So Joseph is but the messenger. The study of dreams was a science practiced in Egypt by scholarly priests and made popular in the New Kingdom by the "book of dreams," as discovered in the Chester Beatty III papyrus. Egyptian sages would teach that, "The dreams of night and day were weapons against destiny." The term employed in the Bible to define these priests was *hartoummin*, a term that corresponds to the Egyptian title of the chief lector in the priesthood, the *kheri-hebet*. They were the ritualists of the famous "house of life," the *per ankh*, a sort of university of theological and scientific activity.

PHARAOH'S DREAM, GENESIS 41:1–36

> After two full years Pharaoh had a dream. He dreamed he was standing by the Nile River. Suddenly, seven nice-looking, well-fed cows came up from the river and began to graze among the reeds. Seven other cows came up from the river behind them. These cows were sickly and skinny. They stood behind the first seven cows on the riverbank. Seven other heads of grain, thin and scorched by the east wind, sprouted behind them. The thin heads of grain swallowed the seven full, healthy heads. Then Pharaoh woke up. It was only a dream.
>
> In the morning he was so upset that he sent for all the magicians and wise men of Egypt. Pharaoh told them his dreams, but no one could tell him what they meant. Then the chief cupbearer spoke to Pharaoh, "I remember a promise I failed to keep. Some time ago when Pharaoh was angry with his servants, he confined me and the chief baker to the captain of the guard's prison. We both had dreams the same night. Each dream had its own meaning. A young Hebrew, a slave of the captain of the guard, was with us. We told him our dreams, and he told each of us what they meant. What he told us happened: Pharaoh restored me to my position, but he hung the baker on a pole." Then Pharaoh sent for Joseph, and immediately he was brought from the prison.

FACING PAGE:

**The seven
cows and the bull**
The first version of the Book
of the Dead appeared at the
start of the New Kingdom.
One of the most important
chapters is the one featuring
seven cows, symbolizing the
seven good consecutive Nile
floods, associated with the
fertile bull.
Maiherperi papyrus,
Eighteenth dynasty,
Egyptian Museum, Cairo

*After he had shaved and changed his clothes, he came in
front of Pharaoh. Pharaoh said to Joseph, "I had a dream,
and no one can tell me what it means. I heard that when
you are told a dream, you can say what it means." Joseph
answered Pharaoh, "I can't, but God can give Pharaoh the
answer that he needs."*

*Then Pharaoh said to Joseph, "In my dream I was
standing on the bank of the Nile. Suddenly, seven nice-
looking, well-fed cows came up from the river and began to
graze among the reeds. Seven other cows came up behind
them. These cows were scrawny, very sick, and thin. I've
never seen such sickly cows in all of Egypt! The thin, sickly
cows ate up the seven well-fed ones. Even though they had
eaten them, no one could tell they had eaten them. They
looked just as sick as before. Then I woke up.*

*"In my second dream I saw seven good, full heads of
grain growing on a single stalk. Seven other heads of grain,
withered, thin, and scorched by the east wind, sprouted
behind them. The thin heads of grain swallowed the seven
good heads. I told this to the magicians, but no one could
tell me what it meant." Then Joseph said to Pharaoh,
"Pharaoh had the same dream twice. God has told
Pharaoh what he's going to do. The seven good cows are
seven years, and the seven good heads of grain are seven
years. It's all the same dream. The seven thin, sickly cows
that came up behind them are seven years. The seven empty
heads of grain scorched by the east wind are also seven
years. Seven years of famine are coming.*

*"It's just as I said to Pharaoh. God has shown Pharaoh
what he's going to do. Seven years are coming when there
will be plenty of food in Egypt. After them will come seven
years of famine. People will forget that there was plenty of
food in Egypt, and the famine will ruin the land. People
won't remember that there once was plenty of food in the
land, because the coming famine will be so severe. The
reason Pharaoh has had a recurring dream is because the
matter has been definitely decided by God, and he will do
it very soon.*

*"Pharaoh should look for a wise and intelligent man
and put him in charge of Egypt. Make arrangements to
appoint supervisors over the land to take a fifth of Egypt's
harvest during the seven good years. Have them collect all*

The seven cows and the bull of the Nefertari burial chamber

Ramses II considered the chapter of the seven cows the most important in the Book of the Dead. The sovereign devoted a whole wall to the episode in the tomb he created for Queen Nefertari. The tableau, symbolic of seven good flood years, was intended to help bring about a successful inundation.

Tomb of Nefertari, Nineteenth dynasty, Valley of the Queens, Western Thebes

the food during these good years and store up grain under Pharaoh's control, to be kept for food in the cities. This food will be a reserve supply for our country during the seven years of famine that will happen in Egypt. Then the land will not be ruined by the famine."

If we analyze the elements inspiring Pharaoh's dream, there are themes consistent with the Egyptian context. There are first the seven nice-looking, well-fed cows, a symbolic animal borrowed from Egyptian thought, which only appears from the New Kingdom onward. Among the vignettes illustrating the many chapters of the Book of Dead of the eighteenth dynasty, the one relating to the seven cows, which are accompanied by the fertilizing bull of the herd, is the most original. It was intended to recall the arrival of the seven floods, seven "good Niles," according to the Egyptian formula. The seven sickly and skinny cows suggest "bad Niles." However, this would have represented a harmful image and bringing it to life would have been dangerous.

Later in the nineteenth dynasty, on a wall in the tomb of Nefertari, the jewel of the Valley of the Queens (facing Luxor), we find the same illustration of seven magnificent, well-fed cows with spotted coats. Their role in this illustration is to express the sovereign's postmortem wish that her soul return each year on New Year's Day with each new flood, and that the flood bring her and the country she is departing eternal fortune in her afterlife. Obviously, in reality, this wish was not easily fulfilled.

The Egyptians were keen observers of nature and noticed that seven successive fulsome floods were often followed by seven more mediocre tides. The same phenomenon can be observed today. However, the new dam prevents the Nile from flooding the whole of Egypt, and the High Dam reservoir feeds Egypt with water throughout the year.

Sometimes a poor tide could give rise to terrible famine. For reasons of superstition, when it came to illustrating funerary texts such as the Book of the Dead, ancient Egyptians were forbidden from referring to the very event they were trying to escape, in both writing and images. At the time when the authors of the Book of Genesis were writing the Book of Joseph, they might have been unaware of the rhythm and cycle of the Nile's tides. Furthermore, certain details in the story demonstrate that the book's authors were outside Egypt when they wrote their texts, and that their memories only retained the effects of climate and harvests, but not the actual tidal regime on which Egyptian directly depended. One detail in particular is worth dwelling on here: the easterly wind that scorches the corn in the biblical account. In Egypt, it was the southern wind, the khamsin, like the sirocco in North Africa, that caused this effect. Clearly, there is confusion here and it is worth noting that Palestine has an easterly wind with similarly devastating effects as Egypt's southerly wind.

The confusion in the recounting of these traditions leads us to believe that the Hebrews had already left the banks of the Nile when these texts were written. They show that their authors based their accounts using memories they themselves had not lived. They would have added to the only Egyptian image of the well-fed cows, the image of the sickly and skinny cows for easier understanding by those who had never witnessed the tidal phenomenon in Egypt.

All these elements—the account of "Potiphar's wife's" adventures, the incident described by the Hebrews, the history of Joseph in Egypt, and Abram's circumcision at the age of seventy-five, after his stay in Egypt—reveal the considerable contribution made by Egypt to the history of the Bedouins, who gradually picked up aspects of the civilization inherited from the wealthier sedentary Egyptians.

PHARAOH'S PROMOTION OF JOSEPH, GENESIS 41:37–49

Pharaoh and all his servants liked the idea. So Pharaoh asked his servants, "Can we find anyone like this—a man who has God's Spirit in him?" Then Pharaoh said to Joseph, "Because God has let you know all this, there is no one as wise and intelligent as you. You will be in charge of my palace, and all my people will do what you say. I will be more important than you, only because I'm Pharaoh." Then Pharaoh said to Joseph, "I now put you in charge of Egypt." Then Pharaoh took off his signet ring and put it on Joseph's finger. He had Joseph dressed in robes of fine linen and put a gold chain around his neck. He had him ride in the chariot of the second-in-command. Men ran ahead of him and shouted, "Make way!" Pharaoh put Joseph in charge of Egypt. He also said to Joseph, "Even though I am Pharaoh, no one anywhere in Egypt will do anything without your permission." Pharaoh named Joseph Zaphenathpaneah and gave him Asenath as his wife. She was the daughter of Potiphera, priest from the city of On. Joseph traveled around Egypt.

Joseph was thirty years old when he entered the service of Pharaoh (the king of Egypt). He left Pharaoh and traveled all around Egypt. During the seven good years the land produced large harvests. Joseph collected all the food grown in Egypt during those seven years and put this food in the cities. In each city he put the food from the fields around it. Joseph stored up grain in huge quantities like the sand on the seashore. He had so much that he finally gave up keeping any records because he couldn't measure it all.

Pharaoh was very impressed by Joseph's analysis of his dreams, and because of Joseph's perspicacity and his acute sense of reality, he entrusts Joseph with one of the most important roles in the kingdom. The list of distinctions and honors is typically Egyptian, as are the qualities required of the country's most important civil servants, starting with the position that Egyptologists have termed the role of vizier, based on studies of the Ottoman Empire. The sovereign rewards him with the royal ring, which would have been engraved with the royal mark, fine linen clothes—a long starched apron perhaps—and gold collar, no doubt the one called *shebiu*. Joseph was also given a chariot with two horses, which underlines his power, almost on a par with that of the king. When out in the streets of the capital, he would have received great public recognition and been respectfully greeted by the Hebrew word *abrak*, which is maybe drawn from the Egyptian expression *ib-ek*, literally "your heart," meaning "homage to you."

Among other language aspects attributed to our hero we should underline the title of "father to Pharaoh" (Genesis 45:8), which was accorded Joseph. The name probably alludes to the Egyptian title of "divine father" and was the ultimate sign of Joseph's assimilation into Egyptian society. Pharaoh had the clear intention of making him an honorary citizen. The name in Egypt would read "Safnath-Paneah," a name whose etymology is highly deformed, but which Professor J. Vergote of the University of Louvain has interpreted as "he who knows things." Furthermore, the king complements this kindness by marrying Joseph to an Egyptian woman of a noble sacerdotal line.

On the basis of these events, Joseph appears as being fully assimilated into Egyptian society as a trustworthy member with a stately role defined for him by Pharaoh. He will act as an Egyptian, ensuring the country's total safety. A logical pause could be made here to mention Joseph's role as a "father" to Pharaoh. However the next stage of the adventure shows to what extent this man of exception seems to have been marked by Egypt, his adoptive country. His good actions in every way, especially the skill with which he became so valuable to Pharaoh, after his brothers' disgrace, makes the adventure worth recalling here. From here to the end of the account, the reader will notice how welcoming Egypt was in return to the first groups of Semites on its territory, giving birth to a people that would go on to become the Hebrews.

THE SONS OF JOSEPH,
GENESIS 41:50–52

> *Before the years of famine came, Joseph had two sons by*
> *Asenath, daughter of Potiphera, priest from the city of On.*
> *Joseph named his firstborn son Manasseh [He Helps Me*
> *Forget], because God helped him forget all his troubles and*
> *all about his father's family. He named the second son*
> *Ephraim [Blessed Twice With Children], because God*
> *gave him children in the land where he had suffered.*

**Preparation
of agricultural land**
As soon as the four months of
the flood were over, Joseph
set out to inspect the land to
ensure it had been prepared
for the sowing period.
Painted relief in the funerary
chapel of Paheri, el-Kab,
Early eighteenth dynasty

Labor
Joseph had the land worked
with a mattock.
Painted relief in the funerary
chapel of Paheri, el-Kab,
Early eighteenth dynasty

Working the plow
Before sowing, Joseph
ensured that all the land was
plowed.
Painted relief in the funerary
chapel of Paheri, el-Kab,
Early eighteenth dynasty

Start of the harvest
The ears of corn were cut
with a sickle. The stalks are
left on the field for the cattle.
Painted relief in the funerary
chapel of Paheri, el-Kab,
Early eighteenth dynasty

Funerary harvest
Women did not work the
fields. This scene represents
the deceased and his wife
laboring to obtain
immortality.
Tomb of Sennedjem,
Nineteenth dynasty,
Western Thebes

Comedy and hard work
Humor was also a feature of
tomb paintings, as this scene
shows. When the master's
visit is announced, everybody
starts working especially hard.
Tomb painting,
Eighteenth dynasty,
Western Thebes

The next stage
Joseph comes to check
if the corn is ready for
the thresher.
Tomb painting,
Eighteenth dynasty,
Western Thebes

Verification by the scribes
Packing up the wheat is
supervised by Joseph's
scribes. It is nearly time to
pay taxes.
Tomb painting,
Eighteenth dynasty,
Western Thebes

THE YEARS OF FAMINE,
GENESIS 41:53-57

*The seven years when there was plenty of food in Egypt
came to an end. Then the seven years of famine began as
Joseph had said they would. All the other countries were
experiencing famine. Yet, there was food in Egypt. When
everyone in Egypt began to feel the effects of the famine, the
people cried to Pharaoh for food. But Pharaoh said to all
the Egyptians, "Go to Joseph! Do what he tells you!" When
the famine had spread all over the country, Joseph opened
all the storehouses and sold grain to the Egyptians. He did
this because the famine was severe in Egypt. The whole
world came to Joseph in Egypt to buy grain, since the
famine was so severe all over the world.*

THE FIRST MEETING OF JOSEPH
AND HIS BROTHERS, GENESIS 42:1–24

*When Jacob found out that grain was for sale in Egypt, he
said to his sons, "Why do you keep looking at each other?
I've heard there's grain for sale in Egypt. Go there and
buy some for us so that we won't starve to death." Ten of
Joseph's brothers went to buy grain in Egypt. Jacob
wouldn't send Joseph's brother Benjamin with the other
brothers, because he was afraid that something would
happen to him. Israel's sons left with the others who were
going to buy grain, because there was also famine in
Canaan.*

*As governor of the country, Joseph was selling grain to
everyone. So when Joseph's brothers arrived, they bowed in
front of him with their faces touching the ground. As soon
as Joseph saw his brothers, he recognized them. But he acted
as if he didn't know them and spoke harshly to them.
"Where did you come from?" he asked them. "From
Canaan, to buy food," they answered. Even though Joseph
recognized his brothers, they didn't recognize him. Then he
remembered the dreams he once had about them. "You're
spies!" he said to them, "And you've come to find out where
our country is unprotected." "No, sir!" they answered him.
"We've come to buy food. We're all sons of one man. We're*

*honest men, not spies." He said to them, "No! You've come
to find out where our country is unprotected."*

*They answered him, "We were 12 brothers, sons of one
man in Canaan. The youngest brother stayed with our
father, and the other one is no longer with us." "It's just
as I told you," Joseph said to them. "You're spies! This is
how you'll be tested: I solemnly swear, as surely as
Pharaoh lives, that you won't leave this place unless your
youngest brother comes here. One of you must be sent to get
your brother while the rest of you stay in prison. We'll see
if you're telling the truth. If not, I solemnly swear, as
surely as Pharaoh lives, you are spies!" Then he put them
in jail for three days.*

*On the third day Joseph said to them, "Do this, and
you will live. I, too, fear God. If you are honest men, you
will let one of your brothers stay here in prison. The rest of
you will go and take grain back to your starving families.
But you must bring me your youngest brother. This will
show that you've been telling the truth. Then you won't
die." So they agreed. They said to each other, "We're surely
being punished for what we did to our brother. We saw
how troubled he was when he pleaded with us for mercy,
but we wouldn't listen. That's why we're in trouble now."
Reuben said to them, "Didn't I tell you not to sin against
the boy? But you wouldn't listen. Now we must pay for
this bloodshed." They didn't know that Joseph could
understand them, because he was speaking through an
interpreter. He stepped away from them to cry. When he
could speak to them again, he came back. Then he picked
Simeon and had him arrested right in front of their eyes.*

In this episode, the author has used a typically Egyptian
oath, alluding to the sovereign: "As surely as Pharaoh lives!"

RETURN TO CANAAN BY JACOB'S SONS, GENESIS 42:25–38

*Joseph gave orders to fill their bags with grain. He put each
man's money back into his sack and gave them supplies for
their trip. After their bags were filled, they loaded their
grain on their donkeys and left. At the place where they*

FACING PAGE, TOP:

Surveyors
After the harvest and the
declaration of the harvest by
the farmers, Joseph sent
surveyors to measure the area
of the harvested land. On the
right, we see a farmer
standing by his boundary
stone as he assures officials
that it has not been moved to
his advantage.
Tomb painting,
Eighteenth dynasty,
Western Thebes

FACING PAGE, BOTTOM:

Grain silos
The granary was replaced by
sugarloaf silos to protect it
from rats. Joseph made silos
obligatory around the
country.
Reconstruction from
a New Kingdom relief

stopped for the night, one of them opened his sack to feed his
donkey. His money was right inside his sack.

He said to his brothers, "My money has been put back! It's
right here in my sack!" They wanted to die. They trembled
and turned to each other and asked, "What has God done to
us?" When they came to their father Jacob in Canaan, they
told him all that had happened to them. They said, "The
governor of that land spoke harshly to us and treated us like
spies. But we said to him, 'We're honest men, not spies. We
were 12 brothers, sons of the same father. One is no longer
with us. The youngest brother stayed with our father in
Canaan.' Then the governor of that land said to us, 'This is
how I'll know that you're honest men: Leave one of your
brothers with me. Take food for your starving families and go.
But bring me your youngest brother. Then I'll know that
you're not spies but honest men. I'll give your brother back to
you, and you'll be able to move about freely in this country.'"

As they were emptying their sacks, each man found his bag
of money in his sack. When they and their father saw the bags
of money, they were frightened. Their father Jacob said to
them, "You're going to make me lose all my children! Joseph is
no longer with us, Simeon is no longer with us, and now you
want to take Benjamin. Everything's against me!" So Reuben
said to his father, "You may put my two sons to death if I
don't bring him back to you. Let me take care of him, and I'll
bring him back to you." Jacob replied, "My son will not go
with you. His brother is dead, and he's the only one left. If
any harm comes to him on the trip you're taking, the grief
would drive this gray-haired old man to his grave!"

JACOB'S SONS LEAVE WITH BENJAMIN,
GENESIS 43:1–14

The famine was severe in the land. When they finished
eating the grain they had brought from Egypt, Israel said
to his sons, "Go back and buy us a little more food."
Judah said to him, "The man gave us a severe warning:
'You won't be allowed to see me again unless your brother
is with you.' If you let our brother go with us, we'll go and
buy food for you. If you won't let him go, we won't go. The
man said to us, 'You won't be allowed to see me again unless

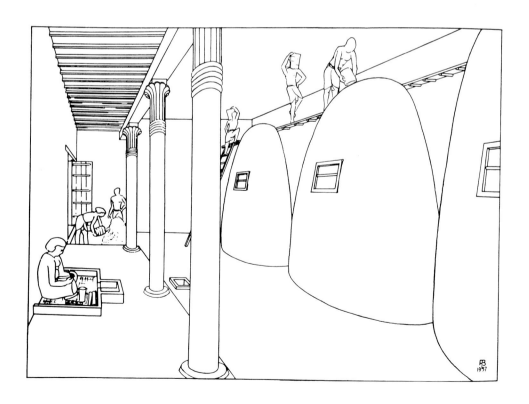

your brother is with you.'" Israel asked, "Why have you made trouble for me by telling the man you had another brother?" They answered, "The man kept asking about us and our family: 'Is your father still alive? Do you have another brother?' We simply answered his questions. How could we possibly know he would say, 'Bring your brother here'?" Then Judah said to his father Israel, "Send the boy along with me. Let's get going so that we won't starve to death. I guarantee that he will come back. You can hold me responsible for him. If I don't bring him back to you and place him here in front of you, you can blame me the rest of my life. If we hadn't waited so long, we could have made this trip twice by now."

Then their father Israel said to them, "If that's the way it has to be, then take the man a gift. Put some of the best products of the land in your bags. Take a little balm, a little honey, gum, myrrh, pistachio nuts, and almonds. Take twice as much money with you. You must return the money that was put back in your sacks. Maybe it was a mistake. Take your brother, and go back to the man. May God Almighty make him merciful to you so that he will send your other brother and Benjamin with you. If I lose my children, I lose my children."

As far as concerns the mode of payment in this text, the use of the terms "money" and "bags of money" must date from a later era, as the accounts are collected from different periods.

At the start of this story, we saw how Joseph was sold for twenty shekels, a currency the Hebrews minted only in the Maccabean period (143–135 BC). But long before, the shekel was already in use in Chaldea and Assyria. In the period of Egyptian history that Joseph's tale takes place, between the Middle and New Kingdoms, no active currency actually existed, only pieces of silver or copper, which were used in exchange for commodities or objects that one might want to buy. Traces have been found in the village of Deir el-Medina, on the west bank of the Nile.

THE ENCOUNTER IN JOSEPH'S HOME, GENESIS 43:15–34

The men took the gifts, twice as much money, and Benjamin. They went to Egypt, where they presented themselves to Joseph. When Joseph saw Benjamin with them, he said to the

FACING PAGE:

Model of Meketre's house
Part of a model showing the rear of a Theban house, overlooking a garden with a sycamore-ringed pool. The roof is fitted with guttering and, beneath the pergola, decorated doors can be seen.
Tomb of Meketre,
Middle Kingdom,
Egyptian Museum, Cairo

man in charge of his house, "Take these men to my house. Butcher an animal, and prepare a meal, because they are going to eat with me at noon." So the man did as Joseph said and took them to Joseph's house. The men were frightened, because they had been brought to Joseph's house. They thought, "We've been brought here because of the money that was put back into our sacks the first time. They're going to attack us, overpower us, take our donkeys, and make us slaves."

So they came to the man in charge of Joseph's house and spoke to him at the door. "Please, sir," they said, "we came here to buy food once before. When we stopped for the night, we opened our sacks, and each man found all of his money inside. So we brought it back with us. We also brought more money to buy food. We have no idea who put our money back in our sacks." "It's alright," he said. "Don't be afraid! Your God, the God of your father, must have given you treasure in your sacks. I received your money." Then he brought Simeon out to them. The man took the brothers into Joseph's house. He gave them water to wash their feet and feed for their donkeys. They got their gifts ready for Joseph's return at noon, because they had heard they were going to eat there.

When Joseph came home, they gave him the gifts they had brought to the house. Then they bowed to him with their faces touching the ground. He asked them how they were. Then he said, "You told me about your elderly father. How is he? Is he still alive?" They answered, "Yes, sir. Our father is alive and well." Then they knelt, bowing down. As Joseph looked around, he saw his brother Benjamin, his mother's son. "Is this your youngest brother, the one you told me about?" he asked. "God be gracious to you, my son," he said. Deeply moved at the sight of his brother, he hurried away, looking for a place to cry. He went into his private room and cried there. Then he washed his face and came out. He was in control of his emotions when he said, "Serve the food." He was served separately from his brothers. The Egyptians who were there with him were also served separately, because they found it offensive to eat with Hebrews. The brothers were seated facing him according to their ages—from the oldest to the youngest. They looked at each other in amazement. Joseph had portions of food brought to them from his table, but Benjamin's portion was five times more than any of the others. So they ate and drank with Joseph until they were drunk.

In the privacy of Joseph's home, the master of the house seems to have adopted the Egyptian way of life. His servants always provide visitors with water for washing their feet, each guest eats separately, seated before a small table, and the host honors his guests by selecting the finest dishes, served individually. This custom still exists in some areas of Egypt.

JOSEPH'S CUP IN BENJAMIN'S BAG, GENESIS 44:1–34

Joseph commanded the man in charge of his house, "Fill the men's sacks with as much food as they can carry. Put each man's money in his sack. Then put my silver cup in the youngest brother's sack along with the money for his grain." He did what Joseph told him. At dawn the men were sent on their way with their donkeys. They had not gone far from the city when Joseph said to the man in charge of his house, "Go after those men at once, and when you catch up with them, say to them, 'Why have you paid me back with evil when I was good to you? Isn't this the cup that my master drinks from and that he uses for telling the future? What you have done is evil!'"

When he caught up with them, he repeated these words to them. They answered him, "Sir, how can you say such things? We would never think of doing anything like that! We brought the money we found in our sacks back from Canaan. So why would we steal any silver or gold from your master's house? If one of us has it, he will die, and the rest of us will become your slaves." "I agree," he said. "We'll do what you've said. The man who has the cup will be my slave, and the rest of you can go free." Each one quickly lowered his sack to the ground and opened it. Then the man made a thorough search. He began with the oldest and ended with the youngest. The cup was found in Benjamin's sack.

When they saw this, they tore their clothes in grief. Then each one loaded his donkey and went back into the city. Judah and his brothers arrived at Joseph's house while Joseph was still there. Immediately, they bowed with their faces touching the ground. Joseph asked them, "What have you done? Don't you know that a man like

Royal reward

The ceremony in which
Pharaoh honored Joseph
would have been similar to
this one featuring General
Horemheb (the future
pharaoh), who is here
depicted receiving beautiful
white linen clothing and
magnificent gold necklaces.
Tomb of General Horemheb
at Memphis,
Eighteenth dynasty,
Currently in the Leyden
Museum, Leyden, Netherlands

*me can find things out because he knows the future?"
"Sir, what can we say to you?" Judah asked. "How else
can we explain it? How can we prove we're innocent?
God has uncovered our guilt. Now all of us are your
slaves, including the one who had the cup." But Joseph
said, "I would never think of doing that! Only the man
who had the cup will be my slave. The rest of you can go
back to your father in peace." Then Judah went up to
Joseph and said, "Please, sir, let me speak openly with
you. Don't be angry with me, although you are equal to
Pharaoh. Sir, you asked us, 'Do you have a father or a
brother?' We answered, 'We have a father who is old and
a younger brother born to him when he was already old.
The boy's brother is dead, so he's the only one of his
mother's sons left, and his father loves him.'*

*"Then you said to us, 'Bring him here to me so that I
can see him myself.' We replied, 'The boy can't leave his
father. If the boy leaves him, his father will die.' Then
you told us, 'If your youngest brother doesn't come here
with you, you will never be allowed to see me again.'
When we went back to our father, we told him what you
had said. Then our father said, 'Go back and buy us a
little more food.' We answered, 'We can't go back. We
can only go back if our youngest brother is with us. The
man won't see us unless our youngest brother is with us.'
Then our father said to us, 'You know that my wife gave
me two sons. One is gone, and I said, He must have been
torn to pieces!" I haven't seen him since. If you take this
one away from me too and anything happens to him,
you'll drive this gray-haired old man to his grave.' Our
father's life is wrapped up with the boy's life. If I come
'home' without the boy and he sees that the boy isn't
'with me,' he'll die. The grief would drive our gray-
haired old father to his grave. I guaranteed my father
that the boy would come back. I said, 'If I don't bring
him back to you, then you can blame me the rest of my
life, Father.' Sir, please let me stay and be your slave in
the boy's place, and let the boy go back with his brothers.
How could I go back to my father if the boy isn't with
me? I couldn't bear to see my father's misery!"*

The gift of a carriage
As a person of higher rank,
Joseph received a carriage
and two horses enabling him
to visit his land.
Tomb painting,
Eighteenth dynasty,
Western Thebes

JOSEPH PRESENTS HIMSELF
TO HIS BROTHERS, GENESIS 45:1–15

*Joseph could no longer control his emotions in front of
everyone who was standing around him, so he cried out,
"Have everyone leave me!" No one else was there when
Joseph told his brothers who he was. He cried so loudly that
the Egyptians heard him, and Pharaoh's household heard
about it.*

*Joseph said to his brothers, "I am Joseph! Is my father
still alive?" His brothers could not answer him because they
were afraid of him. "Please come closer to me," Joseph said
to his brothers. When they did so, he said, "I am Joseph, the
brother you sold into slavery in Egypt! Now, don't be sad or*

angry with yourselves that you sold me. God sent me ahead
of you to save lives. The famine has been in the land for two
years. There will be five more years without plowing or
harvesting. God sent me ahead of you to make sure that you
would have descendants on the earth and to save your lives
in an amazing way. It wasn't you who sent me here, but
God. He has made me a father to Pharaoh, lord over his
entire household, and ruler of Egypt.

"Hurry back to my father, and say to him, 'This is what
your son Joseph says, "God has made me lord of Egypt.
Come here to me right away! Live in the land of Goshen,
where you will be near me. Live there with your children
and your grandchildren, as well as your flocks, your herds,
and everything you have. I will provide for you in Egypt,
since there will be five more years of famine. Then you, your
family, and all who belong to you won't lose everything.'"

"You and my brother Benjamin can see for yourselves
that I am the one who is speaking to you. Tell my father how
greatly honored I am in Egypt and about everything you have
seen. Hurry and bring my father here!" He threw his arms
around his brother Benjamin and cried with Benjamin, who
was crying on his shoulder. He kissed all his brothers and
cried with them. After that his brothers talked with him.

PHARAOH'S INVITATION,
GENESIS 45:16–28

When Pharaoh's household heard the news that Joseph's
brothers had come, Pharaoh and his officials were pleased.
So Pharaoh said to Joseph, "Say to your brothers, 'Load
up your animals, and go back to Canaan. Take your father
and your families, and come to me. I will give you the best
land in Egypt. Then you can enjoy the best food in the
land.' Give them this order: 'Take wagons with you from
Egypt for your children and your wives. Bring your father,
and come back. Don't worry about your belongings because
the best of everything in Egypt is yours.'"

Israel's sons did as they were told. Joseph gave them
wagons and supplies for their trip as Pharaoh had ordered.
He gave each of them a change of clothes, but he gave
Benjamin three hundred pieces of silver and five changes of

clothes. He sent his father ten male donkeys carrying Egypt's best products and ten female donkeys carrying grain, bread, and food for his father's trip. So Joseph sent his brothers on their way. As they were leaving, he said to them, "Don't quarrel on your way back!" So they left Egypt and came to their father Jacob in Canaan. They told him, "Joseph is still alive! Yes, he is ruler of Egypt." Jacob was stunned and didn't believe them. Yet, when they told their father everything Joseph had said to them and he saw the wagons Joseph had sent to bring him back, his spirits were lifted. "You have convinced me!" Israel said. "My son Joseph is still alive. I will go and see him before I die."

THE FOUNDING OF THE PEOPLE OF ISRAEL, AND THE DEPARTURE OF JACOB FOR EGYPT, GENESIS 46:1–7

Israel moved with all he had. When he came to Beersheba, he offered sacrifices to the God of his father Isaac. God spoke to Israel in a vision that night and said, "Jacob, Jacob!" "Here I am," he answered. "I am God, the God of your father," he said. "Don't be afraid to go to Egypt, because I will make you a great nation there. I will go with you to Egypt, and I will make sure you come back again. Joseph will close your eyes." So Jacob left Beersheba. Israel's sons put their father Jacob, their children, and their wives in the wagons Pharaoh had sent to bring him back. They also took their livestock and the possessions they had accumulated in Canaan. Jacob and all his family arrived in Egypt.

Here are cited the names of the children of Israel who went to Egypt.

JACOB'S FAMILY, GENESIS 46:8–27

Altogether, the members of Jacob's family who arrived with him in Egypt, his own issue, not counting the wives of Jacob's sons, numbered sixty-six all told. With Joseph's sons born to him in Egypt, two persons, the members of Jacob's family who went to Egypt totaled seventy.[1]

JOSEPH'S WELCOME,
GENESIS 46:28–34

Israel sent Judah ahead of him to Joseph to get directions to Goshen. When Israel's family arrived in the region of Goshen, Joseph prepared his chariot and went to meet his father Israel. As soon as he saw his father, he threw his arms around him and cried on his shoulder a long time. Israel said to Joseph, "Now that I've seen for myself that you're still alive, I'm ready to die." Then Joseph said to his brothers and his father's family, "I'm going to Pharaoh to tell him, 'My brothers and my father's family, who were in Canaan, have come to me. The men are shepherds. They take care of livestock. They've brought their flocks and herds and everything they own.' Now, when Pharaoh calls for you and asks, 'What kind of work do you do?' you must answer, 'We have taken care of herds all our lives, as our ancestors have done,' so that you may live in the region of Goshen, because all shepherds are disgusting to Egyptians."

THE PHARAOH'S AUDIENCE,
GENESIS 47:1–12

Joseph went and told Pharaoh, "My father and my brothers have arrived from Canaan with their flocks, herds, and everything they have. Now they are in Goshen." ^{2}*Since he had taken five of his brothers with him, he presented them to Pharaoh. Pharaoh asked the brothers, "What kind of work do you do?" They answered Pharaoh, "We are shepherds, as were our ancestors. We have come to live in this land for a while. The famine is so severe in Canaan that there's no pasture for our flocks. So please let us live in Goshen." Then Pharaoh said to Joseph, "Your father and your brothers have come to you. All of Egypt is available to you. Have your father and your brothers live in the best part of the land. Let them live in Goshen. If they are qualified, put them in charge of my livestock." Then Joseph brought his father Jacob and had him stand in front of Pharaoh. Jacob blessed Pharaoh. Pharaoh asked him, "How old are you?" Jacob answered Pharaoh, "The length of my stay on earth has been 130 years. The years of my life have been few and difficult, fewer than my ancestors' years." Then Jacob*

Model of the house at Meketre
A reconstruction of a Theban house, overlooking a garden planted with sycamores. There is guttering on the roof and decorative columns supporting the pergola.
Tomb of Merketre, Middle Kingdom, Egyptian Museum, Cairo

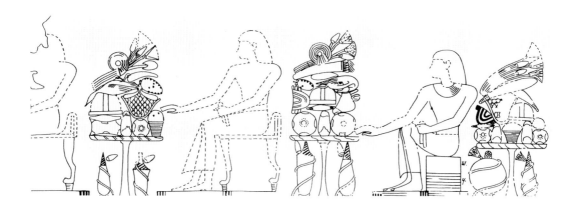

The family meal
In Joseph's spacious abode, members of his family are invited to a meal and served Egyptian style, each sitting in front of a small table.
Drawing in a Theban chapel, Eighteenth dynasty

Servants' tasks
Joseph would have had a large team of servants to make sure his home was clean and fresh. The stone floors were washed daily and visitors' feet bathed in perfumed water.
Tomb painting, Eighteenth dynasty, Tell el-Amarna

blessed Pharaoh and left. As Pharaoh had ordered, Joseph had his father and his brothers live in the best part of Egypt, the region of Ramses. He gave them property there. Joseph also provided his father, his brothers, and all his father's family with food based on the number of children they had.

JOSEPH'S AGRARIAN POLICY, GENESIS 47:13–28

The famine was so severe that there was no food anywhere. Neither Egypt nor Canaan were producing crops because of the famine. Joseph collected all the money that could be found in Egypt and in Canaan as payment for the grain people bought. Then he took it to Pharaoh's palace.

When the money in Egypt and Canaan was gone, all the Egyptians came to Joseph. "Give us food," they said. "Do you want us to die right in front of you? We don't have any more money!" Joseph replied, "If you don't have any more money, give me your livestock, and I'll give you food in exchange." So they brought their livestock to Joseph, and he gave them food in exchange for their horses, sheep, goats, cattle, and donkeys. During that year he supplied them with food in exchange for all their livestock.

When that year was over, they came to him the next year. "Sir," they said to him, "you know that our money is gone, and you have all our livestock. There's nothing left to bring you except our bodies and our land. Do you want us to die right in front of you? Do you want the land to be ruined? Take us and our land in exchange for food. Then we will be Pharaoh's slaves and our land will be his property. But give us seed so that we won't starve to death and the ground won't become a desert." Joseph bought all the land in Egypt for Pharaoh. Every Egyptian sold his fields because the famine was so severe. The land became Pharaoh's. All over Egypt Joseph moved the people to the cities. But he didn't buy the priests' land because the priests received an income from Pharaoh, and they lived on that income. That's why they didn't sell their land.

Joseph said to the people, "Now that I have bought you and your land for Pharaoh, here is seed for you. Plant crops in the land. Every time you harvest, give one-fifth of the produce to Pharaoh. Four-fifths will be yours to use as seed for your fields and as food for your households." "You have saved our lives," they said. "Please, sir, we are willing to be Pharaoh's slaves." Joseph made a law concerning the land in Egypt which is still in force today: One-fifth belongs to Pharaoh. Only the land of the priests didn't belong to Pharaoh. So the Israelites settled in Egypt in the region of Goshen. They acquired property there and had many children. Jacob lived in Egypt seventeen years, so he lived a total of 147 years.[3]

This surprising story is rich in food for thought. It becomes apparent that Joseph's stay in Egypt was not a chance event. Yahweh had deliberately chosen this specific land on the edge of the Nile, midway between Africa and the Near East, so that the intelligence of a young seventeen-year-old peasant, humble guardian of his father's cattle, might flourish. For his exceptional nature to fulfill its destiny, he had to enter the welcoming land of the Pharaohs, establish himself there, and share the Egyptians' existence.

As he initially adapts to Egyptian society, Joseph became close to the country's leaders. Not only did he take over the estate of a man who, according to legend, had bought it as a slave, he also managed to interpret the dreams of the king of Egypt himself. It might well appear strange that a humble peasant could interpret the dreams of the cupbearer and baker. But Yahweh inspired Joseph, and told him to answer skeptics with these words: "Isn't God the only one who can tell what they mean?"

The matter of Pharaoh's fears when he emerges from his nightmare and his inability to understand its message are a

Mosquito net of Hetepheres
The funerary equipment of Hetepheres, the mother of the great Khufu, included a mosquito net. The same model was to be found in the New Kingdom. The wood and gold frame was covered in a veil of fine linen.
Tomb of Hetepheres,
Fourth dynasty,
Egyptian Museum, Cairo

different matter. Again, Joseph is self-negating: "God can give Pharaoh the answer that he needs." However, it is hard to believe that Pharaoh, the supreme master of what is a nameless country in this account, was ignorant of the Egyptian symbol of the seven cows with its direct relationship to the age-old legend of the Nile's tides and their characteristics. For millions of years the river flooded Egypt at a fixed date, on or around July 18, the day the Sothis star, which had remained invisible for seventy days, reappeared at dawn, minutes after and in the vicinity of the sun. When the flood arrived, the New Year returned, the country was renewed and the sovereign, identified with the young sun god, celebrated his birthday.

Pharaoh would have been well versed from an early age in the teachings of the sages, the masters of the "house of life." He must have been only too aware of the protective value of the symbolism of the seven cows, alluding to the seven good tides of the Nile regularly followed by seven poor floods. What bizarre circumstances, therefore, led both Pharaoh and his entourage of advisors to overlook this clear image that the whole of Egypt would have been able to recognize? In my mind there is only one conceivable answer: at the time of the events involving Joseph in

Egypt, the chief of the land must have been a stranger to the country, as yet uninitiated to the special rhythm of its climate.

Joseph, the young peasant, was new to the eastern Delta region where, for some time, Semites—Hyksos no doubt, his Canaanite brothers—had been moving in and settling. When, with the full support of the "foreign" Pharaoh, Joseph saved Egypt and his Canaanite brothers from famine and disaster, the Bible concludes with the descendants of the children of Jacob-Israel settling in the land of Goshen, as indicated by Pharaoh. This might have happened during the mysterious fourteenth dynasty, at the time of the Hyksos occupation of the country.

The nation that Yahweh foresaw constantly grew over two dynasties until the princes of Upper Egypt, concerned about the Hyksos conspiracy with the land of Cush, to the south, undertook to drive them out of the country as they were now seen as occupiers. It was Ahmosis, the "Liberator" and founder of the Theban eighteenth dynasty, who won this war.

However, during this period Egypt had deeply marked the people it had once welcomed onto its soil, especially in its northern province. For centuries afterwards the occupiers benefited from this wonderful legacy.

Riverboat
For his inspections of the country, Joseph would travel from the Delta to southern Nubia in a beautiful riverboat. His cabin was decorated in brightly colored fabric.
Tomb painting,
Eighteenth dynasty,
Western Thebes

XII

Wisdom

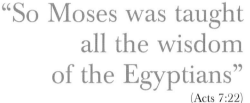

"So Moses was taught
all the wisdom
of the Egyptians"
(Acts 7:22)

When discussing the wisdom of antiquity, reference is often made to the land of the Pharaohs where this precious quality featured highly. The teaching of wisdom, considered a virtue, was called *sebayt*, and was dispensed from father to son, and master to disciple. Very early, it led to the building of a network of power relationships that taught young Egyptians good conduct and discipline, bringing a sense of logic and ethics, essential qualities to Egyptians eager to find the "straight path to God." These teachings were still being dispensed by sages in the latter stages of the ancient Nile civilization.

WISDOM IN THE OLD KINGDOM

Back at the start of the third dynasty, in the Old Kingdom, the divine gift of wisdom was attributed to the scholar Imhotep, architect to King Djoser. None of his writings have been found, but we do know of the existence of a Book of Instructions written by an anonymous contemporary vizier, for the education of the king's son, Kagemni. Then in the 4th dynasty, in the Old Kingdom, there were the Instruction of Hardjedef. But the most famous collection of ethical codes, date from the fifth dynasty: the very popular Instruction of Ptahhotep.

Amenhotep, son of Hapu
This statue represents the great architect and advisor of Amenophis III during his youth.
Karnak,
Eighteenth dynasty,
Egyptian Museum, Cairo

FACING PAGE:
Thoth, the baboon
The hamadryas baboon is native to Ethiopia. Because of its calm behavior, it was associated with meditation, science, and, by extension, the mysteries of the calendar. It was often depicted crowned with a crescent moon.
Glazed terra cotta, gold, and silver statuette,
Early Saite Period,
Musée du Louvre, Paris

Statues of sages
Two of these statues in the temple at Karnak represent Amenhotep, the great architect of Amenophis III, a sage among sages. The son of Hapu, Amenhotep was said to have lived to the age of 110.
Temple of Amun, Karnak, Eighteenth dynasty, Egyptian Museum, Cairo

WISDOM IN THE MIDDLE KINGDOM

In the First Intermediate Kingdom, between the Old and Middle Kingdoms, we have managed to conserve the Instruction of Khety III, written in the tenth dynasty for his son and successor Merikara. These writings became a part of Egyptian daily life, and aimed above all at training students for work in the royal administration and offices.

WISDOM IN THE NEW KINGDOM

The New Kingdom picked up on this tradition. From this period, the Instruction of Ay and the Instruction of Amenemope still survive. They both repeat some past wisdom, but add comments to highlight its ethical quality.

TEACHINGS IN THE LATE PERIOD

In the Late Period, Instructions written in demotic Greek echo
the more elaborate reflections in the Instruction of
Ankhsheshonqy and those of the Papyrus Insinger.

EGYPT AND THE BIBLE

Teachings such as these were developed throughout the
Egyptian civilization, long before the texts of the Bible
appeared. Biblical texts are known to date back to the latter
times of the reigns of David and Solomon (tenth to eighth
centuries BC at the earliest) and without doubt their
inspiration comes from ancient Egypt. Comparisons of
Egyptian and Israeli texts clearly show the similarities
between them, as well as the Israel's receptivity to the
influences of the land of the Pharaohs. It is surprising
that no other ancient civilization produced ethical
texts in such quantity or shared Egyptians' great
preoccupation with the afterlife. Furthermore, the Egyptians
produced teachings that were remarkably appropriate
to their historical juncture, and changed according to
different periods. For example, Prince Hardjedef, supposedly
the son of Kheops, was advised to prepare his burial place,
indispensable to his survival, rather than amass transient
earthly prosperity.

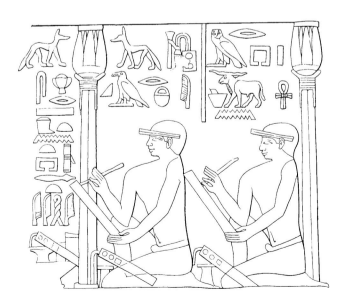

Scribes at work
Scribes were naturally
expected to work in silence,
conducive to intellectual
work. Their office features
columns with closed-bud
capitals.
Tomb decoration,
Fifth dynasty, Saqqara

Woman with a mirror
Prostitute applying make up.
Papyrus,
Twentieth dynasty,
Museo delle Antichità Egizie,
Turin

Drinking goblet
On the same theme, it was
the role of the master to
preach virtue. It was
considered unhealthy to visit
"beer houses" too often, with
their provocatively tattooed
women of loose morals and
free-flowing beer and wine.
Glazed terra cotta, New
Kingdom, Leyden Museum,
Leyden, Netherlands

THE EGYPTIAN IDEAL

In Kagemni's instructions, considerations of correct
behavior for men, from table etiquette to the right posture
when silent (*ger*), could not in any way be neglected.
The need for men to heed this advice was absolute
in order to mark them out from the *shemem*, the emotional,
violent or impulsive.

The Instruction of Ptahhotep, from the sixth dynasty,
concerned all human behavior. It stated the importance of
attention to "good manners." Eloquence was a requirement,
as was the art of listening and respecting silence. All the
essentials of good etiquette were described: trust and
obedience toward superiors, and how to treat inferiors, give
orders, and offer a balanced judgment. Private life in its
entirety was analyzed, covering relations between married
couples, children, and friends.

PESSIMISM

The First Intermediate Period was a time of strife for the
country, marked by extensive internal disorder that affected
Egyptians and their morale. Amenemhat I produced his own
instructions, urging his son to trust no one. After this period

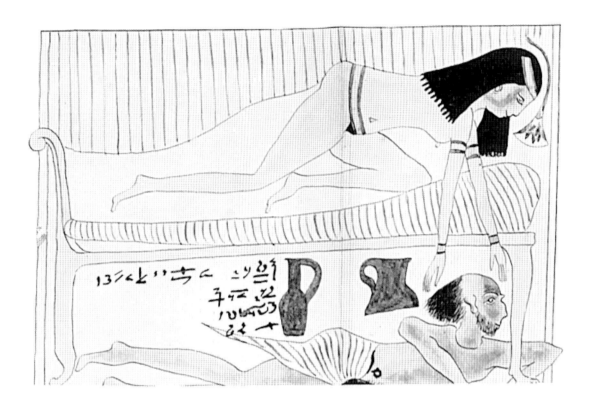

new instructions were written, such as the Hymns to Sesostris III, which, in their great wisdom, taught how the king should be shown the respect he deserved. Among the morality and philosophy, some maxims remained pessimistic, warning of the uncertainty of human destiny.

PSYCHOLOGY

The Books of Wisdom of the New Kingdom were not as accomplished and original as those of previous ages. However, the essential themes were the same, and the Instructions of the Scribe Any and those of Amenemope still insisted on the values of discretion, prudence, and reserve, not forgetting the importance of respect for elders and the fact that god moves in mysterious ways. Finally, the Instruction of Ankhsheshonqy, priest of Ra from the middle of the second century BC, were exceptional in their level of ethical quality.

"Beer house"
When the master addressed his young disciples, he would advise them against frequenting the establishments on the banks of the Nile, where flirtatious hostesses would encourage them to drink too much. (In this depiction, the client is a Semite.)
Papyrus,
Twentieth dynasty,
Museo delle Antichità Egizie,
Turin

Office of the vizier Ay
A glimpse of the interior of an
Egyptian ministry. On the left,
the central aisle of the first
room, flanked by two rows of
scribes, is occupied by the
vizier and his assistants, who
receive orders. In the main
room, the chief minister
worships the patron god of
words and wisdom, Thoth.
Tomb of Ay,
Twentieth dynasty,
Western Thebes

FACING PAGE:
The perfect secretary
In ancient Egypt, a
commoner who heeded the
lessons of wisdom and
behaved correctly in all
circumstances could gain
access to the powerful.
Tomb decor,
Fifth dynasty, Saqqara

EGYPTIAN AND BIBLICAL TEXTS OF WISDOM

Comparing Egyptian texts to certain passages of the Hebrew
proverbs, we can assess the impact of ancient Nile wisdom on
those who founded the Temple of Jerusalem. The Egyptian
texts appeared at fairly regular intervals as we have seen, from
the Old Kingdom to the later periods, from the middle of the
third millennium to the second century BC, while biblical
writings such as Proverbs, Ecclesiastes, and the Book of Kings,
were written between the tenth and eighth centuries BC.

Egypt

Wisdom of Ptahhotep

*Men's plans never come to fruition, but those that God orders
come to pass.*

Wisdom of Any

These plans are one thing, those of the Lord of Life are different.

Wisdom of Amenemope

*It is always in the nature of God to succeed,
Whereas it is always in the nature of humanity to fail.
The words that men say are one thing,
The things that God does are another.*

Instruction of Ankhsheshonqy

The plans of God are one thing,
The thought of man is another.

Israel

Proverbs

The human heart may plan a course, but it is Yahweh who
makes the steps secure.

Egypt

Wisdom of Amenemope

Do not go to excesses in search of gain to ensure your needs.
If your riches come from theft,
They won't last the night with you.
At the break of day, they are not in your home:
You may see their places but they are not actually there.
They are made with wings like geese,
And have flown to the sky!

Israel

Proverbs

Do not wear yourself out in the quest for wealth. Stop
applying your mind to this. Fix your gaze on it, and it is
there no longer. For it is able to sprout wings like an eagle [4]
that flies off to the sky.

SOLOMON: WISER THAN THE EGYPTIANS?

We can see to what extent the wisdom of thousands of years of
Egyptian Instructions affected the great King Solomon. The
Bible declares (1 Kings 5:9–11):

> *"God gave Solomon immense wisdom and understanding, and*
> *a heart as vast as the sand on the seashore. The wisdom of*
> *Solomon surpassed the wisdom of all the sons of the East and*
> *all the wisdom of Egypt. He was wiser than anyone else."*

However, this wisdom departs from the principles
with which God favored him, because later on, and
perhaps under the influence of his many foreign wives,
we read (1 Kings 11:3–21):

"Solomon's heart was not wholly with Yahweh his God as his father David's had been. Solomon became a follower of Astarte, the goddess of the Sidonians, and of Milcom, the Ammonite abomination. He did what was displeasing to Yahweh, and was not a wholehearted follower of Yahweh, as his father David had been. Then it was that Solomon built a high place for Chemosh, the abomination of Moab, on the mountain to the east of Jerusalem, and to Milcom, the abomination of the Ammonites. He did the same for all his foreign wives, who offered incense and sacrifice to their gods. Yahweh was angry with Solomon because his heart had turned away from Yahweh, God of Israel, who had twice appeared to him and had forbidden him to follow other gods; but he did not carry out Yahweh's order. Yahweh therefore said to Solomon, 'Since you have behaved like this and have not kept my covenant or the laws which I laid down for you, I shall tear the kingdom away from you and give it to one of your servants.'"

The chapel of Petosiris
The chapel of Petosiris is a huge building with several rooms. Petosiris, the powerful and wise high priest, was clearly eager to embrace his times. He lived in the period following the easy conquest of Alexandria and had the walls of his "house of eternity" decorated with classic Egyptian bas-reliefs. He also introduced Hellenistic scenes.
Tomb of Petosiris,
late fourth century AD
Tuna el-Gebel, Hermopolis

FACING PAGE:

**Thoth in the form
of an ibis**

The ibis was an incarnation of
Thoth. The animal's long
beak no doubt gave the
impression of a certain skill
with words. In Tuna el-Gebel,
near Hermopolis, an
underground necropolis was
built specially for sacred
mummified ibises and
baboons. On the exterior of
the vessel containing the
mummified ibises, there are
inscriptions alluding to the
"Thrice Great," meaning
"great indeed."

Necropolis of Tuna el-Gebel
Greco-Roman Period

It is time maybe to correct the overconfident statement in
the Book of Kings 2 (5:10), according to which "The wisdom of
Solomon surpassed the wisdom of all the sons of the East and
all the wisdom of Egypt." In the eyes of Yahweh, Solomon was
not so wise! Whatever the case, Gustave Lefebvre is surely
correct when he writes that: "Egyptian wisdom contributed to a
change in Hebrew beliefs about the afterlife. The idea of life
beyond Earth, promised to the devout, was for a long time
foreign to Israel. It appeared in the Maccabean period (second
century BC), when the notion of otherworldly retribution and a
precise idea of immortality took form."

At the end of the indigenous Egyptian dynasties, when
Persian domination was chased out by the arrival of Alexander
in Egypt, Petosiris, high priest of Thoth in Hermopolis,
provides us with the example of a prayer that still survives on
one of the walls of his funerary chapel in Tuna el-Gebel, in
Middle Egypt:

> *He who walks on your path does not stumble. Since I arrived*
> *on Earth, until this day I attained the regions of perfection, no*
> *fault has been found in me.*
> *Oh living! If you listen to my words, if you follow them, you*
> *will see their worth.*
> *The path of he who is faithful to God is beautiful. The one*
> *whose heart is guided there is blessed.*
> *I will tell you what became of me. I will ensure you are*
> *informed of the will of God. I will ensure you penetrate the*
> *knowledge of his mind.*
> *If I have reached the eternal city (the necropolis), it is because*
> *I have done good on Earth and my heart rejoiced in the way*
> *of God, from my childhood to this day. All night, the spirit*
> *of God was in my soul and from dawn I did what he loved.*
> *I exercised justice and I detested iniquity.*
> *I have not associated with those ignorant of the spirit of God.*
> *I did all this believing I would arrive at God after my death,*
> *for I know the day of the Lords of Justice, when they have to*
> *make their judgment.*
> *Oh living! I will ensure you are instructed in the will of God.*
> (Texts from the tomb of Petosiris, nos. 115 and 117).

We are, here, very close to a profession of faith that no
Christian could repudiate.

XIII

Theogamy, the Myth of the Mother Goddess, and the Sacred Bark

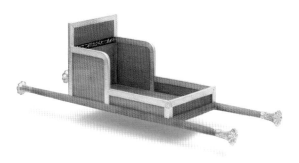

One of Egypt's most dearly held myths is the one where a divinity intervenes as the author of miraculous births. It is a prolongation of a belief that appeared early on in hidden temple writings and paintings, concerning the mystical union of god and mortals.

THE UNION OF GOD AND THE QUEEN

Among all the documents retrieved from excavations, there is no convincing evidence that early ancient Egyptians actually believed in theogamy, unlike many other civilizations. The title "son of Ra" appears for the first time in royal texts from the 4th dynasty (Old Kingdom) placed before the throne name of the sovereign. After the reign of Kheops (around 2550 BC), his successors Djedefra, Khafra, and Menkaura adopted the name of Ra (the sun) in their first names. This demonstrates that the sun creator's name was very closely linked with royal essence. There fortunately does exist one papyrus, the Westcar papyrus, conserved in Berlin, that contains tales of miracles from the reign of Kheops. Even though analysis suggests that the account

Sedan chair
This belonged to Queen Hetepheres, mother of Kheops.
Cedar, ebony, and goldwork, Egyptian Museum, Cairo.

FACING PAGE:
Theogamy, I
The union of Amun, the Hidden, with his chosen one, Queen Ahmose Nefertari, future mother of Hatshepsut.
Relief, eighteenth dynasty, Temple of Deir el-Bahri, Drawing by H. Carter

was written in the Middle Kingdom, a number of details allow us to suppose that the original must date back to the Old Kingdom.

Despite its supernatural subject matter, the text clearly alludes to an historical context and is a highly original, image-laden account, written in the spoken language of the people, with no effort at style. Clichés and repetitions abound, and its vocabulary lacks variation, but it draws the reader into a world until this point unknown in Egypt. It reveals the mysteries of royal births brought about by the intervention of god on a mortal, in this case a wife of a priest of Ra.

The story recounts that, one day, the sons of Kheops were taking it in turns to entertain their father by recounting miracles to him. It was the turn of the Prince Hardjedef, who stood up to speak and said:

You have heard examples of what those who are deceased can do: one does not know truth from falsehood. But there is someone living under Your Majesty, during your own reign, whom Your Majesty does not know and who is a great magician.
His Majesty said: "Who is it, Hardjedef, my son?"
Prince Hardjedef answered: "There is a man named Djedi, who lives in Djed-Snofru. He is a man of 110 years of age, but he eats 500 loaves of bread, the side of an ox for meat and he drinks 100 jugs of beer to this day. He can join a severed head, he can make a lion walk behind him . . ."
Then His Majesty spoke: "You yourself, Hardjedef my son, shall bring him to me."
The ships of Prince Hardjedef were prepared and he traveled southward to Djed-Snofru. Now after that the ships had moored on the banks, he (continued) traveling by land, seated in a carrying chair made of ebony, with its carrying poles made in sesnedjem-wood covered in gold.
Now when he arrived at Djedi's, the carrying chair was set down. He stood up to greet him. He found him, resting on a mat on the threshold of his house, with a servant beside him, anointing him, and another one rubbing his feet. Prince Hardjedef said: "You are as a man who has not reached a grand age. Even though in reality you are indeed old, at the point of death, of being placed in a coffin and of one who sleeps until day, you are free of illness, free of coughing. So greetings, venerable one. I am here to summon you

with a message from my father, Kheops. You shall eat the delicacies that the king gives, the food of those who serve him and he will send you, through happiness, to your ancestors in the necropolis."
And this Djedi said: "In peace, in peace, Hardjedef, son of the king, beloved by his father. May your righteous father Kheops reward you! May he advance your rank among the elders. May your ka prevail over your enemies and your soul know the paths that lead to the gate of Hebesbag. So greetings, Prince."
The Prince held out his hand to help him up. He went with him to the shore, lending him his arm. Djedi said: "Give me one of those barks so that it might bring my children and my writings to me." Two barks with their crews were brought and given to him. Then Djedi traveled north in the boat in which Prince Hardjedef was.
When he reached the court, Prince Hardjedef went in to report to His Majesty the King of Upper and Lower Egypt, the righteous Kheops. Prince Hardjedef said: "Sovereign of Life, Health and Strength, my Lord, I have brought Djedi." And His Majesty said: "Go, bring him to me." His Majesty went into the great hall of the palace and Djedi was sent to him. His Majesty then said: "How is it, Djedi, that I have never seen you until now?" And Djedi said: "It is he who is summoned, who comes, Sovereign. I have been summoned and behold, I have come." Then His Majesty said: "Is it true what people say? Can you join a severed head?" (There follows a moral lesson for the king, and a miracle.)
Then the king Kheops said: "It is also said that you know the number of secret chambers of the sanctuary of Thoth."
Djedi said: "So please you, I do not know the number thereof, Sovereign, my Lord, but I do know the place where they are." His Majesty said: "Where are they, then?" And Djedi said: "There is a box of flint in a room named 'Chamber of the Inventory' in Heliopolis. You may behold it in this box." His Majesty said: "Go, bring it to me!"
But Djedi answered: "Sovereign, my Lord. Behold, it is not me who will bring it to you." And His Majesty said: "Who will bring it to me, then?" Djedi said: "It is the eldest of the children that are still in the womb of Reddjedet who will bring it to you." His Majesty said: "I want it, but who is this Reddjedet?" Djedi replied: "She is the wife of a priest of Ra, Lord of Sakhbu. She is pregnant with three children of Ra, the Lord of Sakhbu. He has said that they shall assume the most excellent office of the entire land and the eldest of them shall be Great Seer in Heliopolis."

Now the heart of His Majesty fell into sadness because of this and so Djedi said: "What is this sad mood, Sovereign, my Lord? Is it because of the three children? I meant to say, first your son, then his son and then one among them." His Majesty said: "When will Reddjedet give birth?" And Djedi said: "She will give birth in the first month of winter, on the fifteenth day." His Majesty said: "Just when the sandbanks of the Two Fishes channel are dry, my servant. Otherwise I would have set sail to her myself, and seen the temple of Ra, Lord of Sakhbu." Djedi said: "Then I shall create four cubits of water on the sandbanks of the Two Fishes channel."
His Majesty went into the palace and His Majesty then said: "Let Djedi be appointed to the house of Prince Hardjedef, so that he shall dwell with him. Make his provisions to be a thousand loaves of bread, a hundred jugs of beer, one ox and a hundred bundles of vegetables."
And His Majesty orders were enacted.

(Westcar papyrus 6:22–8, 10 and 9:1–11:1)

THE BIRTH OF THE KINGS OF THE FIFTH DYNASTY

On one of these days, Reddjedet was having pains and her labor was hard. The Majesty of Ra, Lord of Sakhbu said to Isis, Nephthys, Meskhenet, Heket, and Khnum: "Would that you go and help Reddjedet deliver the three children she is carrying in her womb and who shall assume the most excellent office of the entire land. They will build your temples, they will provide for your altars, they will make your libation tables flourish and they will increase your offerings."

So these gods set out, and changed their appearance to that of musicians and dancers. Khnum accompanied them as a porter. When they arrived at the home of Userre, they found him standing still, his clothes in disarray. They held out their rattles and sistra. And he said to them: "My wife, behold, she is a woman suffering from labor pains." They said: "Let us see her, for behold, we know about childbearing." And he said to them: "Proceed."

They went to Reddjedet, locking the room behind them. Isis placed herself before her, Nephthys behind her, and Heket hastened the birth. Then Isis said: "Don't be so mighty (*Ouser*) in her womb, for your name is *Ouser-ka-f.*"

This child rushed forth onto her arms, a child of one cubit

in length, strong of bones. His limbs were incrusted with gold and his headdress of true lapis lazuli. They washed him, cut his umbilical cord, and placed him on a set on bricks. Then Meskhenet approached him and she said to him, "A king who will assume kingship over the entire land," while Khnum made his body healthy. Then Isis placed herself before her, Nephthys behind her, and Heket hastened the birth. Isis said: "Do not delay (*Sah*) in her womb, for your name is *Sahré*."

The child rushed forth onto her arms, a child of one cubit (in length), strong of bones. His limbs were incrusted with gold and his headdress of true lapis lazuli. They washed him, cut his umbilical cord and placed him on a set on bricks. Then Meskhenet approached him and she said to him: "A king who will assume kingship over the entire land" while Khnum made his body health. Then Isis placed herself before her, Nephthys behind her and Heket hastened the birth. Isis said: "Do not be so dark (*Keku*) in her womb, for your name is *Keku*" (King Kakai).

The child rushed forth onto her arms, a child of one cubit (in length), strong of bones. His limbs were incrusted with gold and his headdress of true lapis lazuli. Meskhenet approached him and she said to him: "A king who will assume kingship over the entire land." And Khnum made his body healthy. They washed him, cut his umbilical cord, and placed him on a set on bricks.

This precious passage recounting the birth of the kings, in the presence of the goddesses, did not appear until the New Kingdom. It was selected by Hatshepsut, as will be seen later, to illustrate her Deir el-Bahri temple. There is no other cited source for this mystery so, in order to represent it so faithfully after so many centuries, the scholarly sovereign must have consulted temple archives. There is no existing Middle Kingdom document either showing signs that the legend was perpetuated. And in the New Kingdom, it might be noted that, in Heliopolis, Ra was replaced by Amun, lord of Thebes. Hence the Creator switched guise, but still survived several millennia to illuminate the birth of the sun king.

It was this great moment of theogamy that the queen elected to use to decorate the exquisitely positioned architectural features of her "Temple of a Million Years" in Deir el-Bahri. She devoted the north side of the second colonnade, directed toward the sunrise and rebirth, to illustrating the event, paying careful attention to the details of its symbolism. In doing so she revealed the mystery to all for the first time.

Theogamy, II
The announcement to the
queue by Thoth, the divine
messenger.
Relief, eighteenth dynasty,
Temple of Deir el-Bahri,
Drawings by H. Carter

Theogamy, III
Khnum, the divine potter,
turns the embryo of the future
Queen Hatshepsut and his *ka*.
Relief,
Eighteenth dynasty,
Temple of Deir el-Bahri,
Drawing by H. Carter

THE UNION

In this way, Hatshepsut restored old beliefs which had
remained veiled beneath secrecy and the dust of ages. Using
magnificent polychrome illustrations, she depicted the essential
stages of theogamy, the union of a god and a mortal.

Hatshepsut evokes another instance. In her temple we see the
outline of Amun (*Imen* = the Hidden) enthroned in his heavenly
residence. He is depicted ordering Thoth, the master of time, to
return to Earth and choose a lady noble and beautiful enough to
receive divine favors. Thoth returns with information appealing
enough that Amun reveals himself on Earth. He appears in the
chamber of the happy elect, Queen Ahmose, where according to
writings he discovers her asleep. The couple encounters each
other in a sober yet unreal setting, marked with innocence and
poetry. Their union is suggested by the image of god and queen
sitting facing to face, as though on a cloud, their knees
interlocking as the two gods of protection, Selkhet and Neith,
support their feet. At the same time, the "Hidden One" presents
the sign of life, the ankh cross, to his lover.

The words uttered by the god, a possible distant echo of the
Song of Songs, are less chaste than the illustrations of the
couple. Amun then holds out another sign of life, to complete

the cycle and bring maximum effectiveness; Queen Ahmose holds out both hands and takes it from him. Not wasting a second, on his return to his universe, Amun calls up Khnum, the divine ram-headed potter, the same potter who fashioned humanity using mud from the Nile, water, and straw. Amun orders him to make him the child he has just conceived, his *ka*, the double that accompanies the king on Earth; other humans only encounter their double after death. To complete the creation, frog-headed Heket breathes life into the young being, then the great god sends Thoth to tell the queen she will give birth to a daughter of god, destined to reign on Earth (the girl is however depicted on the relief by the figure of a boy).

Theogamy, IV
The queen's procession to the delivery room.
Relief, eighteenth dynasty, Temple of Deir el-Bahri, Drawing by H. Carter

Theogamy, V
The delivery bed bearing the queen and the wet nurse. Below, the two cows symbolize the great Hathor and her role in feeding the newborn and his double.
Relief, eighteenth dynasty, Temple of Deir el-Bahri, Drawing by H. Carter

THE ANNOUNCEMENT TO THE QUEEN

Ahmose is stunned by the news. She stands frozen to the spot, arms motionless against her body, almost paralyzed, as she listens to Thoth's prophetic words. There is not a visitor to the temple of Deir-el-Bahri who on encountering the scene does not exclaim: "But it's just like the announcement made to Mary by the angel Gabriel!" Here is yet another biblical source of inspiration for reference during our investigation into origins.

THE BIRTH

After time passes, Khnum and Heket, the patron god of births, join the queen on her journey to the "birthing chamber." In real life, the room was probably painted in ruddle, recalling the color of the pool of the sacred cave of the Valley of the Queens, symbolic of the bloody uterus of the great goddess. The custom was perpetuated through the ages. In ancient Rome, the room where the future master of the country was born might have been covered in red porphyry, from which came the epithet of porphyrogenitus given to the child after his birth.

Back in the invisible world of the divine, two large beds are presented, one on top of the other, instead of side by side. Both are similarly shaped in the form of an outstretched lion, and each decorated with a lion's head, symbolic of the lion's protection. The beds are depicted as overlapping, instead of side by side, and bear the queen and her servants, who were there to help during delivery. As soon as the child appears, Thoth presents him and his *ka* to his divine progenitor, who greets him and recognizes him as his own. At the same time back in the visible world of the royal palace, Queen Ahmose, child in arms, is cared for by the midwives, dedicated to the goddess Hathor. The women bear cows' heads, evoking the milky food received by the divine fetus in his mother's womb. Beneath the delivery bed, there are also two milk cows depicted, assigned to newborn and his *ka*. This milk, this special essence, is designated as *ankh-ouas* and comes from the orb of the solar eye.

REJUVENATION RITES

The birth of the child king obviously corresponded with the appearance of a revitalized sun, alluding to the permanent rejuvenation rites for the year. It will be remembered that New Year is announced by the reappearance of the Sothis star on the eastern horizon, completed by the return of the Nile's flood, the moment when the sovereign's annual jubilee is celebrated.

WHITE NILE, RED NILE

The flood tide, swollen by the water of the equatorial lakes and rivers of Ethiopia, flowed first into the White Nile, carrying with it whitish green plants torn from the banks of the Nile; it then took on the red hue of the alluvium conveyed from the

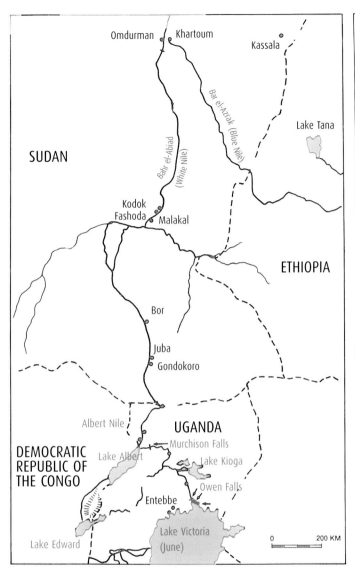

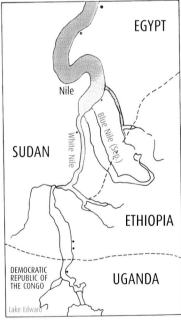

The great Nile
Before reaching Ethiopia, the
waters of the Nile are a
whitish green color. This
water becomes almost red
when its Ethiopian tributary,
the Atbara, flows into it,
bearing ferruginous soil.

The two temples at Abu Simbel
View of the south temple (Meha) and north temple (Ibchek) before they were dismantled and reassembled almost sixty meters higher up.
Nineteenth dynasty, Abu Simbel, Nubia

Atbara, the Ethiopian river that joins the Nile. Then the tidal water reached the mouth of the second cataract, at the gates of Nubia, as though awash with blood, the blood of the goddess (the divine mother) who each year brings to the world the infant sun king, ready to reign over the country throughout the New Year. In the symbolic world, one cannot help but dream sometimes and let one's imagination roam. Sometimes, however, fiction encounters reality this way.

THE ILLUSTRATION OF A MYTH

When Ramses II dug the two caves of Ibchek and Meha, on the site of Abu Simbel, not far from the second cataract, he no doubt did so to reinforce the regular and abundant return of the Nile's fertile waters, so indispensable to Egypt's existence. His intention was also to ensure his own renewal as sovereign, the divine solar child, reborn each year to the great joy of the country. In the thirteenth century BC, the two sanctuaries of Abu Simbel became the architectural symbols of this cosmic and profoundly poetic myth. The ritual consisted of conferring power to the sovereign and his great royal wife, Nefertari, to play the roles of the Sothis star and sun respectively, so that this mystical union would bring about the return of a magnificent annual flood, at this predestined location at the southern Nubian border. To highlight this union, the respective axes of the two sanctuaries joined in the Nile.

NEFERTARI AND THE ROLE OF IBCHEK

The northern cave dug into the mound of Ibchek was destined for the queen; the huge underground temple in the south, meanwhile, dug into the rock of Meha, was to become the majestic cavern of the sun king. The *pronaos* of Ibchek has a wall decorated with a bas-relief with a single focal point, Nefertari herself, in all her juvenile splendor, receiving the crown of Sothis from the hands of Hathor and Isis. This crown, decorated with the high remiges of the royal hawk, is very different to that of Hathor's ostrich feather headdress. Hathor, an image of Eros and love, is placed behind the queen, holding her headdress in place. In front of Nefertari stands Isis, the eternal mother, in a similar pose.

NEFERTARI–SOTHIS

Nefertari is represented walking between the two goddesses toward the exit of the cave to prepare for her appearance. It is also inside the cave of Ibchek, the bosom of the goddess, that the mystery would take shape, engendering the birth of the divine child. To encourage the divine birth, on the other side, facing the "coronation" of Nefertari, there is a scene of the king and queen presenting Taweret (Theoris, patron goddess of births) with bouquets of flowers imploring her to bring about the joyous royal apparition of the New Year. On the wall at the back of the holy of holies in the cave appears the now greatly deteriorated statue of the cow Hathor, charged with returning the rejuvenated king to the world by making him appear before her. In parallel to the image of the king's emergence from the darkness, there are two images of the flood, Hapy, that frame the door, apparently making to leave the sanctuary.

We can trace instances of the Egyptian solar calendar on our own calendar, inherited from that of Egypt. The Sothis star should reappear at the end of the solar year, and with it the

The transformation of Nefertari
Queen Nefertari, principal wife of Ramses II, receives the crown of Sothis, whose horns are adorned with two upright feathers, from the hands of Isis and Hathor.
Painted relief, small temple, Nineteenth dynasty, Abu Simbel, Nubia

Revival of Ramses II
At New Year, Ramses will be reborn to the cow Hathor.
Temple of the queen, Nineteenth dynasty, Abu Simbel, Nubia

Façade of Ibchek
The façade of the sacred cave
features four statues
of Ramses and a pair of
twenty-two-foot monumental
statues of Nefertari.
Small temple at Abu Simbel,
Nineteenth dynasty, Nubia

The two gods of the flood
leaving the holy of holies at
the Ibchek cave.
Small temple at Abu Simbel,
Nineteenth dynasty, Nubia

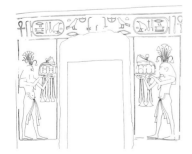

New Year, after twelve months of thirty days, with the addition
of the five epagomenal days. These five days preceding the
star's return were considered a very dangerous period, when
anything could happen: plague, cholera, storms, earthquakes,
or sudden death. According to legend, these were the days
accorded by the Creator to the celestial canopy, the goddess
Nut, after her failing, so that she could give birth to her
forbidden progeny, permitted by divine mercy.

THE PRIMITIVE PLACE OF THE NATIVITY

This offspring made up the Osirian family, with Osiris the first,
then Isis, Nephthys, Seth, and Horus. It is my suggestion that
our Christmas celebration is prefigured in the first of these
days, the three hundred and sixty-first, with the birth of the god
martyr, Osiris, which will be announced by a star, before the
arrival of the flood and the New Year.

MEHA AND RAMSES-SUN

This event is depicted on the façade of the grand sanctuary of
Meha by the statue of the Pharaoh. The sovereign appears
renewed and vibrant, as Horus Horakthy, the fiery hawk-

**The appearance
of Ramses-Horakhty**

Above the narrow door of the
speos (temple) of Meha is an
alcove containing a statue of
Ramses represented as
Horakhty, or "Horus of the
Horizon." He is bearing the
head of the solar hawk.

Great Temple at Abu Simbel,
Nineteenth dynasty, Nubia

Magi of the south

Illustration of the precursors
of the Magi, who arrived from
the south. The dignitaries
brought products from their
regions for the one they freely
recognized as their master.

Magi from the north

Illustration of the precursor
theory of the Magi from the
north. The dignitaries would
freely come to worship and
present gifts to the image of
the reborn king.

Relief from the Great Temple,
at Abu Simbel,
Nineteenth dynasty, Nubia

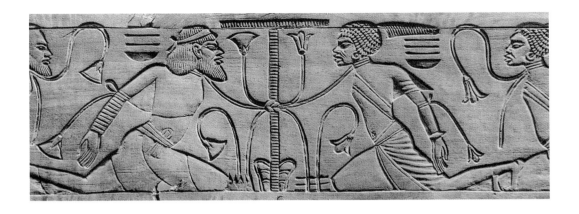

headed Horus of the horizon, like the star that appears on the horizon. Horus dominates the narrow entrance to the great temple, dressed only in his primitive loincloth. He seems to be moving toward the call of the star. His image is flanked by two huge hieroglyphs, which express the dynamism of his mutation into a new sun and that serve to complete his mortuary name, Ouser-Maat-Ra: "Powerful is the living equilibrium of the Sun."

THE MAGI

There is a long frieze, engraved at the base of the façade near the ground, which demands particular attention. To understand its huge importance, it is first worth referring to official scenes where Pharaoh is shown in the company of other ethnic groups, representing different categories of people. The gathering is made up of prisoners, mostly kneeling, with arms and legs tied by stems of heraldic plants from Upper and Lower Egypt. A similar image can be found at the entrance to the grand temple of Meha, with Pharaoh framed by two huge rows of prisoners. In the north, are represented different examples of human "types" from neighboring and distant lands of the Near East. To the right of the entrance corridor we can identify Libyans, Babylonians, Semites, and Hittites, and on the south side, Africans from Sudan and Nubia. There is no figure representing the inhabitants of the land of Punt, "land of the god," land of myrrh and oliban (south west Ethiopia?), who are not depicted as hostile to Egypt. Pilgrims are also in the frieze, arriving freely, peacefully, and respectfully from the outside of the temple. They face the great sanctuary for the celebration of the mystery.

This scene depicts the homage paid to Pharaoh by the free and worthy representatives of neighboring countries to the south and north of Egypt, with whom Pharaoh held peaceful and friendly relations. These dignitaries show no indication of submission or humility. They are kneeling, arms raised toward the temple entrance, with a table of offerings placed before each as gifts for the sun king. This double relief roughly three feet high runs adjacent to the floor and must have been often partly masked by sand accumulated by the wind. The representation, by its special location, seems unique.

It is highly likely that these visitors to the Pharaoh, guided by the miracle star, Sothis, prefigure the Magi; they are a feature of other later religions too, Mazdeism in particular. They bring the breath of universalism to the other symbols in

FACING PAGE, TOP:
Tutankhamun's Stool
By way of a comparison, a classic image of foreign representatives from lands submissive to Egypt. The ties binding them often resemble lily and papyrus stalks.
Eighteenth dynasty, Egyptian Museum, Cairo

FACING PAGE,
BOTTOM LEFT AND RIGHT:
Detail of the statue of Nefertari
On the façade of Ibchek, the queen appears twice wearing the headdress of Sothis.
Small temple at Abu Simbel, Nineteenth dynasty, Nubia

The bark of Amun
During a procession, the sacred bark of Amun is worshipped by Ramses II himself.
Stele, nineteenth dynasty, Egyptian Museum, Cairo

FACING PAGE:
Ramses II escorts the bark of Amun
After the ceremony marking the New Year and the arrival of the flood, the sacred bark of Amun leaves Abu Simbel. On route to Egypt, the bark is first welcomed by the king at the temple of el-Derr. The king then escorts it to the Nile in the direction of the other sanctuaries before reaching Egypt.
Temple of Ramses in el-Derr, Nineteenth dynasty, Nubia

the two temples, similar to that of the "good news." (See the second chapter of the Gospel according to Saint Matthew, the only one to allude to the Magi.)

THE SACRED BARK

The great vessel bearing Amun was due to leave from the rock-cut temple of Meha. Amun, the powerful spirit hidden in the river, who had to transport the rejuvenated image of the god-king, was placed high on his pedestal, at the feet of the four statues of this holy of holies. Here, Ramses was flanked by Amun, Harmakhis (Hor-em-akhet, or "Horus in the horizon"), and Ptah, the obscure. Ramses was thus guarded by the divine forms governing the sun (Horakhty), flood (Amun), and latent hidden strength (Ptah).

Long before, in the eighteenth dynasty, Ramses' predecessors in the New Kingdom, Thutmose III, Amenhotep II, and Thutmose IV, had evoked and revered

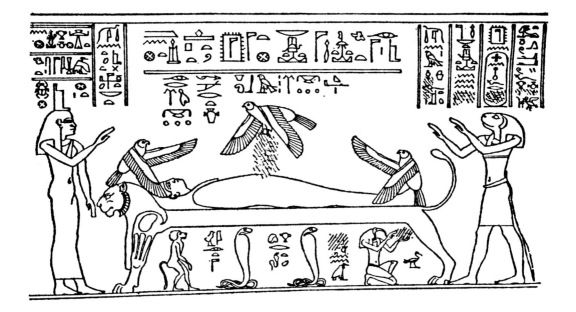

Funerary bed
Representation of the
funerary bed of Osiris, on
which he was brought back to
life by the bird of Isis so that
he could impregnate her.
Greco-Roman Period,
Philae

the divine bark in the Nubian temple of Amada. They had
given it life with the figures of Horatkthy and Amun, seated
side by side. Their worship was also evoked on the walls
of the chapel, by the reverence paid both to the sun and
the form of Amun.

After founding the miraculous sanctuaries of Abu Simbel
devoted to his deified body and the mystery of Nefertari-
Sothis, to complete this work, Ramses build three majestic
sanctuaries dedicated first to Horakhty, then Amun, and
finally Ptah, along the course of the sacred bark before it
arrived at the Egyptian Nile. These temples were the
Hemispeos temples of Derr, Wadi es-Sebua, and Gerf
Hussein. The bark finally came to embody the flood itself
and followed the path traced by the water spreading over
metropolitan Egypt. Ramses made sure to build sanctuaries
along the Nubian river, which could receive the sacred craft,
celebrate its arrival, and bring it closer to the ground on
which the water would spread. These consisted principally
of the temples of Derr, Wadi el-Sebua, Gerf Hussein, and
Dakka. The vessel would then sail on to join its famous
metropolitan shelter in Thebes.

THE AWAKENING OF OSIRIS

At the end of the Pharaonic dynasties, the myth
of the flood and the renaissance of the god-king at the New
Year were seen to rely on the provisional resurrection of
Osiris to release the divine seed. We know that the righteous
god, victim of the evil Seth, had been dismembered and
thrown into the Nile, where the Oxyrhynchus fish, or
sturgeon, swallowed his genitals; this, naturally, prevented
him from procreating. On the walls of Greco-Roman
temples, a highly secret scene appeared showing Osiris on
his funerary bed.

The god's generative flame is rekindled by the work of
Isis, the magician, transformed into a bird. Isis wakes
Osiris from his torpor using the wind produced by her
beating wings. While we are on the subject, we read in the
Gospels according to Saint Matthew (1:18) that "This is how
Jesus Christ came to be born. His mother Mary was
betrothed to Joseph; but before they came to live together
she was found to be with child through the Holy Spirit";
this is the virgin, or *parthenos* of the text of Greek tradition
(Isiah, 7:14).

Mammisi of Philae
West side of the *mammisi*
("birth house") in the temple
of Isis on Philae.
Island of Philae,
Greco-Roman Period

Isis pregnant
The goddess is depicted against a background of papyrus, symbolizing the maternal waters, or amniotic fluid. Her child is thus still in its fetal state. Isis is protected by Thoth and Amun.
Relief, *mammisi* at Philae, Greco-Roman Period

**Appearance
of the royal child**
Divine birth of the royal child and his *ka*, or double.
Relief, *mammisi* at Philae, Greco-Roman Period

PHARAOH, SON OF THE GODDESS

At the end of the Pharaonic era, during the last stage of its thousand-year adventure, the myth of the god's renaissance was transformed slightly as different contemporary sets of beliefs merged, acquiring new secret elements, which were often borrowed from Osirian legend. Others too seem to have been redrafted, without losing sight of the essential message.

The reliefs on the walls of *mammisis*, small temples devoted to theogamy, still evoke the miraculous birth of the king. In them, Pharaoh is still interpreted as the sun-child; he is Horus, but also Ihy, the son of Hathor. He is no longer brought into the world by the great royal wife, however, but included as the son of Isis, the great sorceress, who could not have been impregnated by her husband in his lifetime. The glory of Isis won over the popular domain, whereas in the secrecy of the *mammisis* she is portrayed as a crouching figure holding her god-child who is set to reign over humans.

BIRTH OF THE YOUNG GOD AND HIS KA

In the pyramid of the first pylon of the Greco-Roman temple of Philae leading to the *mammisi* are sculpted certain stages of the

divine birth, which are either reminiscent of the standard myth, or modify the classical scenes in some way. In the lower panel, against a background of papyri, we find the birth of the two cows of Hathor. With more than a thousand years between them, the two cows recall the two nursing cows, represented on the delivery bed of the Queen Ahmose, mother of Hatshepsut. In the upper panel, we witness the scene of the birth, portrayed by symbolic images intended to be in harmony with the composition.

Above the two cows, we see a rectangular pool of water, from which appear two magnificent blooming lotuses, the floral source of the morning sunrise. On each of their calyxes, the small naked god Ihy, and his double (his *ka*) illustrate the appearance of the great star emerging from the flower. These two small figures are reminiscent of the birth scene of the future Queen Hatshepsut.

ISIS, THE SEAFARER

Venerable Egypt remained faithful to the symbolism of the divine bark. Later on the sacred craft became the symbol of the return of the errant Hathor, but also of her appeased form, the

Birth of Horus
Isis protects her divine child, who appears at the sound of the harp at the New Year.
Relief, *mammisi* at Philae, Greco-Roman Period

The bark of Isis

In the first courtyard of the great temple can be seen the bark of Isis, guided by her own priests and not the bark of Amun.

Relief, Temple of Isis, Philae, Greco-Roman Period

divine mother Isis. From early times, the legend was intricately linked with the Nile's cycle, its flood, but also the rhythm of the seasons that the river commanded. I believe I have developed an explanation of this that serves both practical and geographical purposes. The river's cycle, which determined the seasons, was compared to the behavior of a desirable maiden, a dream princess, living at the court of her father, and the sovereign of the land was dependent on her as a source of happiness. Despite the joy around her, which also depended on her presence, one day she ran away to the far south. Nothing more was heard of her and Egypt slipped into depression. The court was desperate. One day, the king caught wind of where she had gone and sent messengers after the Distant Goddess; the messengers never returned.

Bereft of the light of his life, the sovereign sent out the smartest of his ambassadors, Thoth's monkey. The monkey received a hostile reception from the daughter, now transformed into a lioness, surround by her family of cubs. After many fruitless attempts, Thoth managed to entice her back to the border of her fatherland, level with the first cataract, charming her with a thousand and one tales (which were often resurrected by European storytellers later). Thoth made the most of the moment's hesitation from the Distant Goddess and pushed her into the Nile. The lioness became the gentle cat Bastet, protector of the home. She brought back prosperity to the land and palace, as well as the New Year, the return of the flood. The Distant Goddess is symbolized in the return of the vessel.

Returning from Nubia, the bark later contained in its *naos* the statue of the goddess, who was later confused with Isis and paraded by priests on the island of Philae, as can be seen on one of the pylons of the temple there. Aloft on the priest's shoulders, it returned to its elegant annual refuge, Trajan's kiosk. Hailed in prayers and worshipped by the people, and even the Roman legionaries garrisoned in the south, the goddess's bark, bedecked in flowers, was escorted by its followers to the northeast of the Delta.

Isis pharia
The statuette of Isis, patron of seafarers, carrying an anchor and the child-god, or horn of plenty. Isis first appeared in this form in the northeast of the Delta after the construction of the lighthouse of Alexandria.
Bronze, Alexandrine Period, Musée du Louvre, Paris

ISIS LACTANS AND ISIS PHARIA

When Alexander arrived in Egypt, the effigy of Isis, as *Isis lactans,* the divine mother of the universe with child on her lap, was sometimes switched with that of *Isis pharia*, the beam of light that protected and welcomed sailors into the newly built port of Alexandria. The goddess is represented holding a horn of plenty in her hand (or sometimes the solar child); in the other hand, she is holding a sea anchor. The images rapidly spread across Mediterranean shores. For example, overlooking the monastic necropolis of the Lérins Islands in the hills around Cannes in the South of France, the church of Le Suquet has a statue of the Virgin Mary holding an anchor. From the Mediterranean, the image of Isis even illuminates the hazy horizons of mainland France. The silhouette of the saintly seafarer still haunts the reliefs of the chapels of ancient Pannonia, where she features floating on a frail skiff of which

The Virgin of Le Suquet
This golden statue recalls the antique images of Isis of the Lighthouse that were brought to the French coast by seafarers. Mary is depicted bearing an anchor and the infant Jesus.
Nineteenth century,
Le Suquet church, monastic cemetery, Lérins Island

Coat of arms of Paris
The former coat of arms of Paris, recalling the emblem of the boatmen of Lutetia. The Egyptian bark is decorated with figureheads of Osiris and Isis on the prow and stern. The Sothis star shines over the image of Isis, seated on her throne. On the right is a statuette of Osiris.
Nineteenth century,
Archives of the Hôtel de Ville, Paris

she is holding the sail. In Rome, Pompeii, and Herculaneum, and many other cities besides, she was central to famous rituals. She even landed in Gaul, where she was found among the ferrymen of Lutetia, of whom she became the patron goddess. She also appeared on Paris's archaic coat of arms, and in Brittany, her boat—the boat of the Saintes Maries de la Mer—still sails in a yearly local fishing festival.

THE SEAFARER IN KRAKOW, AND ELSEWHERE

Forty years ago, I arrived in Krakow on Corpus Christi. I easily imagined myself transported to the banks of the Nile during the celebration of the divine mother, the worship of whom has influenced many other forms of worship. On the way to the cathedral, the focus of the ceremony, the sacred boat containing the statue of the Virgin Mary, was carried aloft by its most fervent believers. The path taken by the procession was strewn with flower petals, and the statue, bringer of protection, clearly recalled that of the supreme goddess, who now conveyed the whole of divinity.

The accumulation of so many clues cannot be the result of coincidence. The sources of other religions do not render such clues. Egypt underwent many trials and tribulations in the final years of its ancient history. When Alexander liberated Egypt from the Persians in 333 BC, the conqueror's successors, the Ptolemaic kings and Macedonian generals, quickly drained the intellectual elite from the Near East to the new city of Alexandria, or Alexandria ad Aegyptum as it was called at the time. The city was far removed from the Nile environment.

THE JEWS AT ELEPHANTINE

Meanwhile, out of the gaze of museums and philosophers, the country had been welcoming a large and flourishing Jewish community into its midst. The Jewish immigration took place before and after the capture of Babylon and focused on the city of Elephantine, where it seems the first synagogue was created, long before the idea reached Jerusalem. The building was accompanied by a school, in keeping with the Egyptian custom that located places of learning near temples, as well as the essential fountain, or *sybil*.

A Greek version of the Hebrew Bible, the Septuagint, was produced by the Jewish community of Alexandria in the third BC under the patronage of Ptolemy II Philadelphus (285–240 BC), for which it was claimed that seventy scholars worked for seventy days.

JEWISH BELIEFS IN THE SECOND CENTURY B.C.

It was only from the second century BC that Egyptian wisdom really contributed to Hebrew beliefs relating to the afterlife. The doctrine concerning the immortality of the soul did not appear before the second century BC (Genesis 7:10), while the Pharaonic theme of the balance of judgment only turned up later in Jewish writing (Enoch 4:1, 61–82). In the era when Christianity was expanding in Egypt, Isis with her child Horus naturally turned into the Virgin Mary holding the Baby Jesus on her knee.

Isis lactans
The classic statuette of the divine mother, Isis, breastfeeding her child, Horus. The fact that the child has not actually taken her breast indicates that the goddess is awaiting the birth of the heir of Osiris.
Bronze, Ptolemaic Period, Musée du Louvre, Paris

XIV

The Secret
of the Sanctuaries

This swift overview can in no way claim to have covered all facets of the Egyptian spirit and its influence. But it is not hard to see the degree, variety and quality of its heritage, a heritage that much of humanity owes to its ancestors.

There have been two subjects central to our appreciation: the solar calendar and the creation of the alphabet, both sources of so much potential and knowledge. But we are indebted to this civilization in many other areas. We have examined architecture, writing, and medicine, which Hippocrates exploited extensively, but above all ancient Egyptian wisdom, which was renewed and reinforced from dynasty to dynasty, enabling people to improve and develop.

Nile dwellers had a remarkable gift for observation. It encouraged them to use the image and the behavior of their animals to create a symbolic language that was not only relevant to their lives, but which has also crossed centuries and frontiers. Their symbolism was easy to decipher as it was always used with such precision. We looked at the game of goose and Horus as Saint George, and these are just two examples among so many others that have been adopted,

Tomb of Petosiris
Petosiris was the high priest of Thoth. Reading the texts on the walls of his chapel, near Hermopolis, we can be sure that he was well qualified to pass on the most exalted of traditions.
Chapel of Petosiris,
Fourth century AD,
Tuna el-Gebel

added to, or amended, but which have been exported out into the world without major transformation, something that might have made them impenetrable.

No one can dispute the great qualities of the early Egyptians. As the Bible says: "So Moses was taught all the wisdom of the Egyptians." "Wisdom is the product of Egypt," declared one prince of Byblos. The country was much admired by its neighbors, but it was with its closest neighbors, the Hebrews, that contact was most sustained.

The history of Joseph at the court of Pharaoh provides a vivid example, based on lived experience and memories. The effect of Egyptian civilization on Israel is obvious. In return, the Bible was the first book of "modern times," long before hieroglyphs were deciphered. Through the saga of Joseph, it gave us a gripping glimpse, albeit limited and embroidered, of life in Egypt in its most classical period. The Bible was the first history book to even mention Pharaoh.

We have been able to trace, over the final Pharaonic dynasties, to what extent Osirian belief supplanted other kinds of moral discipline and metaphysical concept. All that remained to do was identify the principles related to Isis's influence that inspired the adoption of a new faith based on love of one's fellow man. The terrain had been prepared by the suffering endured by Egypt throughout successive invasions, relayed by Roman domination.

In the city of Alexandria, great minds tackled philosophy, while in the depths of Egypt people were weighed down by taxes, but were otherwise ignored by the occupiers. However, some venerable lords of Middle and Upper Egypt continued to model their existence around the Osirian myth, which had become a genuine popular religion in the country. It was a belief to which even the "everyday" occupiers adhered, the modest colonists, legionaries, and mercenaries from abroad, who were better treated on the edge of the Nile than in Rome.

In the heart of Middle Egypt, Petosiris, high priest of Thoth in Hermopolis, near Tell el-Amarna, declared as the country was welcoming Alexander, in 333 BC: "If I have reached the eternal city, it is because I have done good on Earth and my heart rejoiced in the way of God".

Petosiris's thinking was not new, whereas the Hebrews' concept of "sheol" only contained a trace of belief in the afterlife. At the start of the second millennium BC, an Asyut prince had engraved on the wall of his tomb: "The thought was always in my mind that I would reach God on this day of death." In these words, we can see how there was no need for any intermediary between Egyptian thinking and the early Christian religion. The seed had already been sewn on the banks of the Nile since "the time of God." To my great satisfaction, one of my rare courageous colleagues wrote a sentence which now seems indisputable: "It was the Egyptian religion that paved the way to Christianity." Wherever Christianity reached, the worship of Osiris, then Isis, preceded it by several centuries, leveling the terrain, preparing minds to welcome the universalist teachings of Christ.

Christianity did not need the Hebrew religion to be introduced into Egypt. There was no need for this agent because, from its origins, Egypt had already showed signs of Christian thinking. The fraternity, humanism, and legendary wisdom of this dialogue is inescapable, and they seem to materialize in the response of the elder Djedi to Pharaoh, when he was asked to cut off the head of a prisoner of war, then to stick it back. The old man displays the courage that characterized the Egyptian conscience: "No! Not with a human being, Sovereign, my Lord! It is forbidden to do such a thing to the cattle of God!" (Papyrus Westcar, Old Kingdom).

However, when it comes to nascent Judaism, when the Bible tells the story of Moses on Sinai and the Ten Commandments, we discover a general imperative law and instructions revealing a mentality much different to that of Egypt. Here is a selection of the terms of the Decalogue:

> *You will have no gods other than me.*
>
> *You must not make yourselves any image or any likeness of anything in heaven above or on earth beneath or in the waters under the earth; you must not bow down to these gods or serve them. For I, Yahweh your God, am a jealous God and I punish the parents' fault in the children, the grandchildren and the great grandchildren, among those who hate me.*
>
> *You must not misuse the name of Yahweh your God, for Yahweh will not leave unpunished anyone who uses his name for what is false.*
>
> *Labor for six days, doing all your work, but the seventh day is a Sabbath*
>
> *Honor your father and your mother, as Yahweh your God has commanded you, so that you may have long life.*
>
> *You must not kill.*
>
> *You must not commit adultery.*
>
> *You must not steal.*
>
> *You must not give false evidence against your fellow.*
>
> *You must not make gods of silver to rival me, nor must you make yourselves gods of gold.*
>
> *And whoever strikes down a human being will be put to death.*
>
> *If further harm is done, however, you will award life for life, eye for eye, tooth for tooth, hand for hand, foot for foot, burn for burn, wound for wound, stroke for stroke.*
>
> *If an ox gores a man or woman to death, the ox will be stoned and its meat will not be eaten, but the owner of the ox will not be liable. But if the ox has been in the habit of goring before, and if its owner has been warned but has not kept it under control, then should this ox kill a man or woman, it will be stoned and its owner put to death.*
>
> *The man who has intercourse with an animal will be put to death*
>
> *You will not ill-treat widows or orphans.*

This is a glimpse of the Ten Commandments (Deuteronomy 4:45–11:33), the laws and customs that Moses proclaimed for the sons of Israel on their exit from Egypt, when beyond the River Jordan: "Yahweh made this covenant not with our ancestors, but with us, with all of us alive here today. On the mountain, from the heart of the fire, Yahweh spoke to you face to face."

Meanwhile in the heart of Egypt, from the early Middle Kingdom, we find the program of charity to be applied by all believers inscribed on funerary stelae: "I gave bread to the hungry, water to the thirsty, clothes to the naked, a bark to a person without. I made offerings to divine forms and funerary offering for the fortunate."

If we review the range of qualities required to be considered a worthy and righteous man, we only have to consult chapter 125 of the Book of the Dead, dating back to the start of the New Kingdom, where the deceased confesses and presents his purity to the forty-two gods present before Osiris at the balance of judgment:

> *I have committed no evil upon men*
> *I have not oppressed people*
> *I have not wrought evil in the place of right and truth*
> *I have never attempted to know what there isn't to know*
> *I have not blasphemed God*
> *I have not defrauded the poor of their property*
> *I have brought about no evil*
> *I have not done what the gods abominate*
> *I have not cause harm to be done to a servant by his master*
> *I have not caused pain*
> *I have caused no man to hunger*
> *I have made no one weep*
> *I have not killed*
> *I have not given the order to kill*
> *I have not inflicted pain on anyone*
> *I have not stolen the food offerings in the Temples*
> *I have not sullied the bread of the gods*
> *I have not been a pederast*
> *I have not fornicated in the holy places of the god of my city*
> *I have not diminished the bushel when I've sold it*
> *I have not diminished the land*
> *I have not encroached on land*
> *I have not added weights to the scales*
> *I have not stolen milk from the mouths of children*

I have not spied
I have not gossiped
I have only argued about my own business
I have kept no company with a married woman
I have not fornicated
I have not inspired fear
I have transgressed nothing
I have not let my words carry me away
I have not been deaf to words of truth
I have not been insolent
I have not polluted myself
I have not been false
I have not insulted
I have not been brutal
I have not been dazed
I have not transgressed my condition and lost temper with God
I have not gossiped
I have brought about no evil
I have not insulted the king
I have not made noise
I have not blasphemed God
I have only enriched myself with my goods

We have no Egyptian document to suggest that a certain Isaa, "the man from Nazareth," in the Galilee of the Nations, undertook to teach the people of Egypt charity, tolerance, clear-sighted kindness, and love of their fellow men. These were values they had always lived by. However the land of Judah was very close to Egypt, and Jerusalem enjoyed relations with its neighbor, the city of Memphis.

Baptism scene
Sovereigns and civilians alike were often represented in their funerary chapels receiving this essential purification. Two spirits baptize the deceased with the ankh sign conferring eternal life. The holy water is depicted by a continuous stream of signs of life (ankh).
Sarcophagus decoration, New Kingdom

THE FLIGHT TO EGYPT

How can we forget the Holy Family's flight from Egypt to escape Herod's cutthroats? The event only features in the Gospel according to Matthew. Was it a real event or only symbolic? And symbolic of what? This gives rise to another question: why did the Holy Family choose to go south, to Egypt, whereas it would have been quicker and less dangerous to travel to a nearer country to the east or north?

The first answer to this question was proposed by Professor el-Assiouty several years ago. The professor suggested that

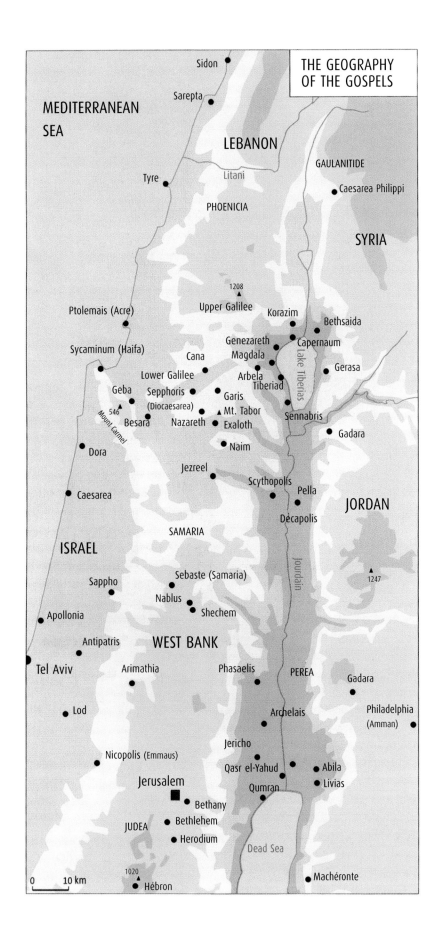

THE GEOGRAPHY
OF THE GOSPELS

MEDITERRANEAN
SEA

LEBANON

GAULANITIDE

Sidon

Sarepta

Tyre

PHOENICIA

Caesarea Philippi

SYRIA

Litani

1208

Ptolemais (Acre)

Upper Galilee

Korazim

Bethsaida

Sycaminum (Haifa)

Cana

Genezareth

Magdala

Capernaum

Lake Tiberias

Gerasa

Geba

Lower Galilee

Arbela

Tiberiad

Sepphoris
(Diocaesarea)

Garis

Sennabris

546

Mount Carmel

Besara

Nazareth

Mt. Tabor

Exaloth

Gadara

Dora

Naim

Jezreel

Scythopolis

Pella

Caesarea

Decapolis

JORDAN

SAMARIA

ISRAEL

1247

Sappho

Sebaste (Samaria)

Nablus

Shechem

Apollonia

WEST BANK

Antipatris

Tel Aviv

Arimathia

Phasaelis

PEREA

Gadara

Lod

Archelais

Philadelphia
(Amman)

Nicopolis (Emmaus)

Jericho

Jerusalem

Qasr el-Yahud

Abila

Bethany

Livias

JUDEA

Bethlehem

Qumran

Herodium

Dead Sea

0   10 km

1020

Hébron

Machéronte

263

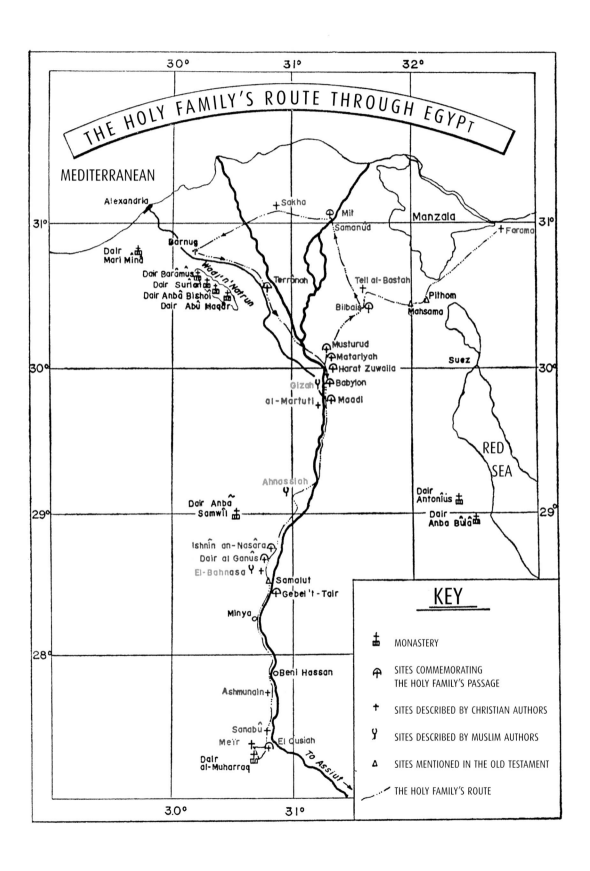

THE HOLY FAMILY'S ROUTE THROUGH EGYPT

MEDITERRANEAN

Alexandria

Sakha

Mit

Manzala

Samanûd

Faramâ

Barnug

Dair
Mari Mina

Wadi'n'Natrun

Dair Barâmus
Dair Suriani
Dair Anbâ Bishoi
Dair Abû Maqâr

Terrânah

Tell al-Bastah

Bilbais

Pithom

Mahsama

Musturud
Matariyah
Harat Zuwaila
Babylon
Maadi

Suez

Gizah
al-Martuti

RED
SEA

Ahnassiah

Dair
Antoníus

Dair Anbâ
Samwîl

Dair
Anbâ Bûla

Ishnîn an-Nasâra
Dair al Ganûs
El-Bahnasa

Samalut
Gebel 't-Tair

Minya

Beni Hassan

Ashmunain

Sanabû

El Qusiah

Meïr

Dair
al-Muharraq

To Assiut

KEY

🏛 MONASTERY

⊕ SITES COMMEMORATING
THE HOLY FAMILY'S PASSAGE

✝ SITES DESCRIBED BY CHRISTIAN AUTHORS

Ɏ SITES DESCRIBED BY MUSLIM AUTHORS

Δ SITES MENTIONED IN THE OLD TESTAMENT

–·–·– THE HOLY FAMILY'S ROUTE

**Map of the route
of the Holy Family**
This map was drawn up by
Father Meinardus and
indicates the positions of the
churches, built to
commemorate the passage of
Jesus (Upper and Middle
Egypt).

**The Tree of the Holy
Virgin**
This is all that remains of the
tree beneath which the Virgin
Mary is said to have sat in
Matariya, near Heliopolis,
during her journey through
Egypt. Only one live branch
survives, its shoots lovingly
tended by the Copts.

Jesus' family could have been of Egyptian origin, like many
other farming families of this rich region, the Galilee of the
Nations. Was the Holy Family returning to its roots?

Egypt seems to have retained its memory of these events
through the Tree of the Holy Virgin in Matariya (Heliopolis),
which is still religiously cared for today. The tree
commemorates Mary's flight with Jesus and is believed to have
been replanted several years before the second century AD.
We should also take into account the places where the Holy
Family might have stayed, where small churches were erected.
Their trail stops to the south of Meir, in Middle Egypt, and at
least seven sites are mentioned in the Coptic writings.[5]

The flight into Egypt was the source for a host of local
myths based on miracles supposedly caused by the presence of
the infant Jesus. The most impressive was reported in the
Arabic Gospel of the Infancy of the Savior, picked up again in
the Gospel of Pseudo Matthew, where it was described with
detailed commentary. We also find it related later in the work
of French fourteenth-century nobleman Jean de Berry, *Les
Petites Heures*. According to the tale, when the Holy Family
entered a temple near Heliopolis, all the statues of idols fell
from the altar. The moment was so impressive that the
governor Aphrodisias arrived with a huge escort to "becalm

and worship the one who had such power over the gods." According to different sources, the Holy Family's stay[6] in Egypt lasted three, five, or seven years (see Jacobus de Voragine's *Golden Legend*). Then the angel ordered Joseph to leave Asyut and return directly to Nazareth in Galilee.

WHY THIS SILENCE?

If the question of how this legacy was passed on to Egypt cannot be answered, we might ask the question why no trace of the new faith appeared there for more than two centuries after the death of Christ. Egypt was still worshipping Isis, but continued to place its aspirations in the complete divine Osirian family: god-father, Isis-mother, and Horus-child, born of a miracle and heir to the ancestral theogamy. This "trinity" was later transformed by the teachings of the Christian Church.

THE TEMPLES, GOD, AND GODS

We should first distinguish between two essential types of temple:
—The great sanctuary where priests worshipped the divine force, essential to maintaining the creative source (for example the Great Temple at Karnak in Thebes).
—The mortuary temple, also called the funerary temple, where the divine energy given to the king as the earthly emanation of the Creator was celebrated and renewed. Here, sanctuaries may have been dedicated to a specific divine form or reserved for royal worship. These temples did not, strictly speaking, have a funerary function comparable to the mortuary chapels of individual owners' burial chambers. They were places where beliefs were celebrated regularly during festivals and at the king's annual jubilee, his ritual regeneration.

Queen Hatshepsut was a real innovator in this area, creating an exceptional temple at Deir el-Bahri. It is also worth mentioning the earlier temple of Mentuhotep in the eleventh dynasty, to the south of the stone corrie chosen by the queen. However, it is the originality, force, and elegance of the queen's monument that really stands out, with its multiple levels, from the first courtyard to the top terrace where the niches and *naos* devoted to the worship of Amun and the royal family were cut out of the rock. The tiered façade and pillars of the three levels give the monument a unique upward movement and aerial

Flight of the Holy Family to Egypt
The event was often commented on in Egypt at the beginning of the Christian era.

The family of Osiris
Horus, the posthumous son, is represented with his mother, flanking the image of Osiris, who has left the mortal world. Gold and lapis lazuli (the inlay of Isis's headdress has disappeared).
Triad of Osorkon, twenty-second dynasty, Musée du Louvre, Paris

Bay's prayer
Example of popular beliefs
A worker at the royal
necropolis by the name of
Bay asks Amun to answer his
prayers. On his stele are
represented "the ears that
hear his prayers."
Engraved stele,
Eighteenth dynasty,
Deir el-Medina

The king burning incense
During religious ceremonies,
burning incense was essential
to ensure purification.
Generally frankincense from
the land of Punt was used.
Tomb painting,
Eighteenth/nineteenth dynasty,
Western Thebes

elegance. Enclosed by a perimeter wall less than two feet high,
it is an architectural creation visible by and for all. Classical
Egyptian temples were designed as fortresses surrounded by
high walls that only people working there could enter. Thus,
people were not able to admire or understand the decorations
on temple walls, and the secrecy around worship was
maintained. However, worship also happened in public
sometimes, taking place outside temples during major
festivities. Statues of divinities were transported and protected
in the *naos* of the sacred bark carried aloft by priests. The
curtains of the *naos* were open during its itinerary and the
crowd could see the precious image within.

Day to day, it seems that people would worship their god
wherever they were, a little like Muslims today. We have proof
of this from the sides of the Theban mountains during the New
Kingdom when the inhabitants of the region would form small
primitive chapels from a handful of stones so as to pray to the
Creator.

So what actually went on inside Egyptian sanctuaries? What
secret rituals were carried out to maintain divine energy and
revive its power, without which the world would crumble?
Firstly the *netjer* was effectively worshipped daily. The closest
translation for *netjer* is possibly "god"; it is a word that is
applied to all the many essential manifestations of nature
which, for the Egyptians, governed its forces. This religion was

not mystical but physical and, according to A. Piankoff's analysis, strangely echoed, or rather inspired, the ideas of Heraclites of Ephesus. These forces that made up the Universe were, notwithstanding, highly structured, and had to revitalize themselves from the ultimate source, the Creator. Rituals ensured that the Creator conserved his powers and did not disappear.

It seems outdated to continue to consider these human forms with animal heads covering temple walls as gods. They simply constituted different expressions of the divine. Their attributes distinguished their particular role in the vast divine machinery; they were energies at work in the conservation of the Universe. There were a number of gods in the public domain, but also and above all God, whom É. Drioton has called the God of the Sages, designated in the sacred writings as the "One and Unique."

Furthermore, when in the Book of the Dead (chapter 125), apparently written in the early New Kingdom, we read that God searches the mind and tries the heart of every man according to the fruit of his doings, a phrase picked up later in Apocalypse, we can be sure that the intention of writers, in this case, was to refer to the One and Unique sublime divine force.

AN EARLY CHRISTIAN RITUAL?

To address these issues, it is worth sounding out possible echoes in neighboring rituals and Pharaonic worship. Before the Late Period, the most common scenes presented on temple walls illustrated the eternal dialogue between the divine being and Pharaoh. Figurative acts were essential, such as offerings from sovereigns to guarantee, in return, the god's generous protection and his eventual intervention. Several times a day, the dialogue was continued. But the determining moments came at sunrise and sunset, when the god awoke and went to sleep.

PROVOKING THE GOD'S APPEARANCE

At sunrise, the critical moment is when the orb appears. It is very probable that the image of the sun springing from its lotus, an image that was very prevalent in later periods, was already used in the oldest temples, but had not yet been popularized. This scene is widespread and illustrated by a magnificent half-open lotus, on the calyx of which appears a crouching solar

Gulbenkian stele
This votive stele, conserved in the Museu Calouste Gulbenkian in Lisbon, is inscribed with this idea from the Book of the Dead echoed in the Book of Revelation: "God searches the mind, and tries the heart of every man according to the fruit of his doings."
Stele, late eighteenth dynasty, Museu Calouste Gulbenkian, Lisbon

Harpocrates on the lotus
The royal child, like the child of god, is represented being brought into the world by the sacred lotus.
Relief,
Temple at Kalabsha,
Ptolemaic Period,
Nubia

**Tutankhamun
reborn from the lotus**
The young king's funerary equipment included this symbolic image of the deceased's rebirth: the head of the sovereign is depicted emerging from a lotus evoking the child-Horus, Harpocrates.
Treasure of Tutankhamun,
Eighteenth dynasty,
Egyptian Museum, Cairo

child, one finger to his mouth or a similar gesture. In the funerary treasure of Tutankhamun, the sun that made the lotus open was replaced by the head of the young king. Elsewhere, the priest is depicted facing east and is seen lifting a chalice similar to the one found at the eastern door of Tutankhamun's burial chamber. In this way, the renascent sun appeared above the flower in a moment of divine illumination, comparable to the communion of the priest at the moment of the Eucharist.

I presented this calcite calyx from the prince's treasure at the Tutankhamun exhibition in the Petit Palais in Paris. The then president of France, General de Gaulle, seemed extremely surprised by the association of the lotus and chalice, raised by the priest at mass to the host, comparable here to the sun. The general immediately commented on the idea to Madame de Gaulle, who was greatly moved at this unexpected and distant connection.

All details of objects used in worship have disappeared, and we can only imagine the essential moment and confine ourselves to the image of Pharaoh or the high priest raising the lotus toward the divine image by its stem. Several collections, however, including the one in Hildesheim, possess an object corresponding to that used in the supreme rite. The object is a hollow metallic stem capped by a closed lotus composed of many white lotus petals (*nefer*), with a cord attached to its base that passes through the stem of the flower. When you pull the cord, the lotus opens to reveal at its heart the infant Horus, crouching with a finger in his mouth. It is with this system that the priest greeted the arrival of the day and paid homage to the celestial light (in the storerooms of the Department of Egyptian Antiquities at the Louvre there are several bronze sections of this precious object).

THE "COMMUNION" OF AMENHOTEP IV AND NEFERTITI

It is my impression that this final act of communion has been conserved by some bas-reliefs discovered in the city of Akhetaten, "the horizon of the Orb" (Tell el-Amarna). We know that the reforming sovereign, Amenhotep IV Akhenaton, rather than offend his entourage, wanted to deconstruct the rites, so that they could be understood and his convictions could be shared. In doing so, his aim might well have been to reveal the secrets of the divine religion, which was generally celebrated in secret in the holy of holies of the solar temple.

Among all his innovations, he had the audacity to depict secret scenes of worship on the walls of his great temple. The scenes he portrayed today bare a close resemblance to those of the Eucharist. There is the image of the sun with rays in the form of outstretched arms presenting the king and Nefertiti with the sign of life (*ankh*), irradiated by Aten. The sovereigns are accompanied by three of their six daughters. The two sovereigns are partaking in the sacrifice of the service, the presentation of the royal offering. Reaching as high as possible,

Chalice of Tutankhamun
This magnificent chalice is in the shape of a blooming lotus. It was placed at the foot of the entrance to the king's tomb to enable him to reappear like the sun on the morning of his resurrection, brought into the world by the sacred flower.
Treasure of Tutankhamun, Eighteenth dynasty, Egyptian Museum, Cairo

"Communion" of the sovereigns of Amarna
Akhenaten and Nefertiti both hold up to the solar orb the supreme offering, a double casket in the name of the solar progeny, Shu.
Tomb relief,
Eighteenth dynasty,
Tell el-Amarna

each presents a casket (a pyxis perhaps) in the form of a double cartouche. On each cartouche are engraved the names and epithets of the Creator, the sun and its manifestation, Shu, the breath of the sun: "Horakhty who rejoices on the horizon in his name of Shu which is in the solar orb."

As with many artistic creations, every detail of the composition is important. There are two ribbons at the base of the sovereigns' headdress, the white crown of Upper Egypt for the king, and the red crown of Lower Egypt for the queen. These ribbons do not fall naturally over the sovereigns' backs; instead they float horizontally. Thus depicted, in the celebratory moment of the sovereigns' dialogue with the divine spirit, this clear evocation of the wind blowing expresses the presence of the air god, Shu, "who is the pupil of the solar eye." This intense life is striking to the viewer and eventually only the effect of the wind blowing is visible. (I don't think this aspect has been noticed by the specialists of the Amarna period.)

The event shown is indeed the supreme sacrifice which, up to the reign of the reformer, was not to be divulged. The comparison with the Christian church service is too clear not to point out. No doubt thousands of years later, the words "This is my body, this is my blood" were added.

PAPAL POMP AND CEREMONY

There are other images in temples and tombs that enable us to imagine what might have influenced papal ceremonies at the time when Christianity was officially becoming established. No doubt, Saint Peter's heirs borrowed something of ancient Egyptian rituals.

In the New Kingdom, we notice that on important occasions the sovereign would be carried on his throne, the feet of which were placed directly on the poles borne by Libyan or Cushite porters. One of the most vivid representations probably alludes to the coronation of Horemheb, where the king, presented to the admiring crowd, is surrounded by huge fans made of ostrich feathers.

When Saint Peter paraded in Saint Peter's Square all those many years ago, he is reported to have been sitting on his *sedia gestatoria*, the feet of which were also placed on poles held aloft by the Swiss Guard. He was also surrounded by servants holding fans of ostrich feathers similar to those of the Egyptians. The comparison is striking.

We know that to restore life to people who had undergone transformation in ancient Egypt it was necessary to complete the ceremony of the "Opening of the mouth and eyes" over the deceased's image. The priest officiated over the mummy before

Akhenaten in procession on his throne
Note the way the royal throne is carried on poles.
Tomb relief,
Eighteenth dynasty,
Tell el-Amarna

Horemheb in procession on his throne
The throne of Horemheb, like that of Ramses later, is carried aloft by bearers, placed directly on poles.
Relief,
Eighteenth dynasty,
Gebel el-Silsila

Double casket
The ritual casket featuring the name of Tutankhamun was discovered in the funerary equipment of the young king.
Funerary treasure
of Tutankhamun,
Eighteenth dynasty,
Egyptian Museum, Cairo

Fan with ostrich feathers
The comparison with the fans in the papal procession is striking.
Painted relief, tomb of one of the sons of Ramses III (Amunherkhepshef),
Twentieth dynasty,
Valley of the Queens

Papal procession, Saint Peter's Square, Rome
The pope's *sedia gestatoria* was carried in a similar fashion on poles.

the great journey commenced, in the same way as he revived newly completed statues. It is maybe not so surprising to note that when the sovereign pontiff is assigned this supreme responsibility, he too carries out the "Opening of the mouth and eyes" on the elevated one. Many other aspects could be highlighted here: the three papal crowns, decorated with *uraeus*, sometimes adorn Amenhotep IV Akhenaton's headdress on the reliefs of temples at Akhetaton. Another key aspect was visible recently at the funeral of Pope John Paul II. The deceased pope was entombed in three successive sarcophagi, as was the case with kings of the New Kingdom, at least if we base our facts on the funerary equipment of Tutankhamun, and on an ancient detailed drawing found in the tomb of Ramses IV. I will also add that ribbons were attached to the royal headdress, from Amenhotep IV Akhenaton onwards, and generally were always worn behind the white crown of Upper Egypt.

EARLY CHRISTIANS AND THEIR PLACES WORSHIP
There are many other examples of these surprising comparisons to be cited. But it is also worth looking at early Christian worship in Egypt. The overriding factor here is the poverty in which Christianity developed. This was true for the early anchorites, who appeared in Upper Egypt and mainly in the rocky desert on the left bank at Thebes.

Today we still encounter in the rocky zones of the Theban desert, on the left bank of the Nile, traces of hermit dwellings that were essentially natural caves, crudely set out in the limestone mountains. Sometimes a small stone wall was all that protected the entrance at night from wild animals such as hyenas and wolves. Sometimes these men of desert solitude, who would sporadically visit the faraway villages of the plain for food, would take refuge from the mountain's freezing winter nights in the burial chamber of the Valley of the Queens, which had been looted even before the end of the New Kingdom. Tombs in the valley are still marked by the graffiti of their childish fantasies. With the arrival of Christianity, these walls were covered by primitive Christian motifs, which transformed the Ramesside royal ladies' underground chambers. The first Christian graffiti of which we know was drawn over the walls and hieroglyphic inscriptions of the queens' vaults. Large crosses appeared made of plants and branches and accompanied with the inscription, "I am the wood of life."

The lack of suitable material obviously affected the construction of religious foundations. So most Pharaonic temples were partly transformed into churches. The most spectacular example was the great temple of Isis in Philae. In this particular sanctuary, the two religions were in direct rivalry and there were even bloody battles.

Often the Pharaonic decorations were hammered out or covered in plaster and replaced with holy images and crosses.

Papal enthronement
Among the ritual ceremonies of the pope's enthronement is the "Opening of the mouth and eyes." In ancient Egypt, this ceremony was intended to bring the mummy to life before it was placed in the burial chamber. It was also carried out on statues before they were displayed.
Tomb of Tutankhamun,
Eighteenth dynasty,
Western Thebes

Ceremonial jar
This beautiful jar capped with a cross was used to transform a temple devoted to the worship of Amun into a Christian church. I discovered it under the former pharaonic altar when the temple of Wadi el-Sebua was dismantled.
Temple of Wadi el-Sebua,
Nineteenth dynasty,
(Ramses II)

Archangel
This image was painted on a wall of the temple at Wadi es-Sebua, and has been partially covered with hieroglyphics.
Temple of Wadi el-Sebua
Painting from the Christian era,
Ramses II,
Nineteenth dynasty,
Middle Nubia

Saint Peter
The main alcove in the temple of Wadi el-Sebua, which may have contained statues of Amun and Ramses, was modified in the Christian era. It was covered in plaster and decorated with the image of Saint Peter receiving the eternal homage of Ramses II.
Nineteenth dynasty
and Christian era

Sometimes only the figure of the god was masked and substituted for the new object of worship, while the ancient Pharaonic setting remained the same. This is how, in the great hall of the Temple of Amun, in Wadi el-Sebua in Nubia, two huge figures of Ramses came to offer flowers to Saint Peter, the new occupant of the temple.

After the second century, monasticism took root in Egypt. The movement was given credence by its many convertees, such as Saint Onuphrius, from Koma in Middle Egypt, who adopted a name formerly give to Osiris: *unen nefer*, "perpetually rejuvenated."

There was also Saint Anthony who was born around AD 251. But the most famous Egyptian monk was Saint Pachomius, born in Upper Egypt at the start of the fourth century, near Esna. His term in the Roman army over, he was demobilized to Thebes. After being baptized, he became a disciple of the hermit Palaemon (around AD 330). He went on to found a community near the town of Akhmim and laid down detailed rules for daily life. He created eleven such communities governed by cenobitic monastic rules. The monastic movement is strictly of Egyptian origin. Its heritage represents the greatest contribution that Coptic Egypt made to Christianity.

Temple of Wadi el-Sebua
View of the second pylon.
The great doorway of
pharaonic times was
considerably reduced in the
Christian era by the creation
of a double doorway.
Originally constructed under
Ramses II (nineteenth dynasty),
Middle Nubia

Great Temple of Isis
In the Late Period, religious
ceremonies were dominated
by the worship of Isis. The
first great temple devoted to
the wife of the deceased
Osiris is to be found at Philae,
where the Nile enters Egypt.
Philae,
Greco-Roman Period

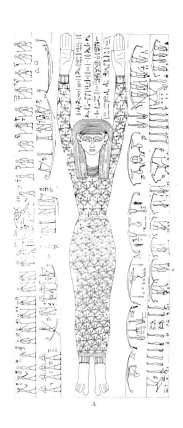

A

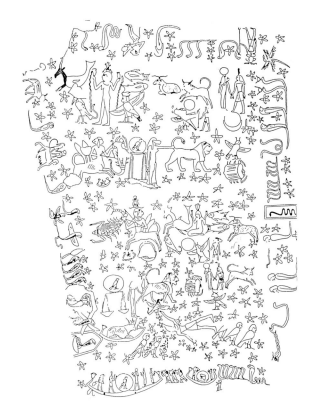

Nut, the celestial vault
The interiors of sarcophagus lids were decorated with images of Nut, the celestial vault, depicted as a woman, her body covered in stars with five points.
Sarcophagus,
Ptolemaic Period,
Musée du Louvre, Paris

Signs of the zodiac
In the Ptolemaic Period, pictograms of the signs of the zodiac appeared on the ceilings of burial chambers, sometimes in disordered fashion.

BIRTH OF THE ILLUSTRATED ZODIAC

For several centuries after Christianity in Egypt, illustrated papyri propagated images of Egypt in the West, mainly through travelers and pilgrims returning from the monasteries of Saint Pachomius. Among these many illustrations, we have found some displaying the signs of the zodiac.

The signs of the zodiac appeared in the Late Period, but Egyptians did not know them in the order they were first presented. Each sign represented concepts of Egyptian symbolism, which were mostly not linked to each other. The signs were used as ceiling decoration and then as ornamentation on the inside of sarcophagus lids. They were depicted flanking the body of a woman her arms raised above her. The woman was the Nut, the celestial vault and wife and sister of Geb, the Earth. Nut, as we have seen, had been separated from Geb because they disobeyed the orders of the Creator. To become the celestial vault, Nut bent her body and pressed down on the Earth with her hands and feet. She is found decorating Greco-Roman temple ceilings in this position.

From the Middle Kingdom, on the insides of the lids of rectangular wooden sarcophaguses appeared astronomical images depicting the solar calendar. The logical extension of this decor appeared in the New Kingdom. The astronomical ceiling decoration of the Ramesseum, the mortuary temple of Ramses II, is one miraculously conserved example. Resplendent with images of constellations and names of solar months, it is crowned in the north by a long thin band of figures and letters indicating the twelve months of the year.

In the Late Period, priests used this illustration as one of the many decorations of mummy sarcophagus lids. In an attempt to translate the circles and figures of calendars by vivid imagery, they decided in the Greco-Roman period to assist the deceased on their path to the afterlife by appealing to ancient symbols from remote sacred temples, rather than use the names of the twelve months of the solar year as a basis for the illustrations.

For this reason, the celestial vault, Nut, is to be found on the inside of sarcophagus lids, as the image of a woman, legs and arms stretched, looming over the mummy in his cask, ready to embrace him. At chest level and on each side of the body, symbolizing the ecliptic, the twelve signs of the months of the year were divided on each side into two series of six signs. The signs held their own individual meaning in the astronomical order, and recalled in the clearest manner possible the characteristics of each month.

The Egyptians used the same ancient distribution of months as their forefathers, and followed the same reasoning when they corresponded New Year with the reappearance of the Sothis star on the eastern horizon. The reappearance of the star coincided with the imminent sunrise and the almost immediate return of the flood, around July 18.

Above the head of Nut, solar symbols still highlight the heat zone. Furthermore, solar symbols parallel with the chest of Nut figure the signs illustrating the hottest months of the year. However, on either side of the sky goddess's feet there are pairs of signs signaling the coldest months of the year.

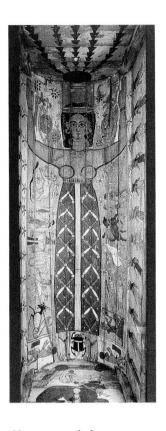

Nut surrounded by signs of the zodiac
This slightly later variation depicts Nut with her arms raised and body surrounded by the twelve signs of the zodiac, in two rows of six.
Sarcophagus of Soter, Greco-Roman Period, British Museum

BELOW, FACING PAGE,
AND PAGE 282:
**The arrangement
of the signs of the zodiac**
A selection of signs of the
zodiac from burial chambers
and sarcophagi of the
Ptolemaic Period.
(See also Chapter I, "The
Calendar").

THE SIGNS AND THEIR SYMBOLS

Let us take one of the best-preserved examples, painted on the
inside of the sarcophagus lid of Soter, conserved at the British
Museum in London. On the bottom, at the left of the feet,
there are the symbols of the last two months of the winter-
spring season (*peret*), symbols that we recognize as Aquarius
and Pisces. Then there are the four signs corresponding to the
four months of the summer season (*shemu*), which complete the
half-year and include the signs of Aries, Taurus, Gemini, and
Cancer. Then we reach the hottest months of the year, at the
end of July, a time when the Creator created an empty space,
for the five epagomenal days, enabling the birth of the Osirian
family. Then the cycle continues with Leo, Virgo, Libra, and
Scorpio, the four months of *akhet*, the period of the flood. Then
we find ourselves back at the first two months of the *peret*
season, the coldest months of the year, symbolized by
Sagittarius and Capricorn.

It now remains to grasp the relation between each month and
its associated illustration in Egyptian symbolism. It will be
remembered that the succession of signs follows the legend of
the god Osiris's transformations in his eternal victory over death.

Aquarius, the first sign of the cycle, is generally depicted
carrying a papyrus stalk on her head, symbolizing the two
mythical sources of the Nile. Maybe the geographers and
hydrologists sent by Queen Hatshepsut to the land of Punt
pushed their exploration further south and differentiated what we
now call the White Nile and the Blue Nile. These two sources
were then represented spurting forth from two libation vases.

Pisces was the small *inet* fish, *Tilapia nilotica*. In
iconography, the fish is always represented alone, but in the
Ramesside period we see the deceased fishing two fish,
representing his "soul of today and yesterday." This is why the
Pisces sign represented two *inet*, attached by a double line, as it
still does today. The deceased, who is due to return with the
flood, but who is still held in the primordial waters, is
represented by this river dweller.

Aries was not the ram of Khnum, master of the cataracts at
his potter's wheel, but the ram of Mendes, from the sanctuary
located to the east of the Delta. The breath emanating from his
nostrils gives air to the fishlike fetus of the future sun, enabling
him to transform his gills into lungs and be reborn, wailing,
into the open air.

Taurus was actually the bounding veal calf born from the womb of her great mother, the celestial Hathor.

The sign of **Gemini** represented the inseparable twins Shu and Tefnut, the Creator's two children, who represent the radiant force of the sun, transmitting it to the deceased as he emerges from the darkness.

Cancer, the scarab beetle, pushes its ball of dung containing eggs due for hatching, which will appear in the world like the nascent star. The beetle is the image of the reappearance of the sun at the start of the world, and of perpetual transformations of the being, who is revived and reborn through himself.

With **Leo** we cross the center of the twelve signs at the moment when the sun, at its zenith, shines over the world. It is the sacred moment when the flood appears in Egypt, heralded by the Sothis star in the pale dawn sky. The symbol of the lion is powerful; it represents the sun at its hottest. The sign is placed on the snake representing the flooding river that both announces and conveys its arrival. Osiris, victim of the evil Seth, is returned momentarily to the light of day by the force of Ra.

Virgo is represented by Isis holding the ear of wheat, symbolic of Seth's act of violence. Osiris is barely reborn when he is once more victim of his dreaded brother's machinations, which will bring about the new death of the god. Fortunately, Isis is watching over the stricken seed, which will be subsequently reborn, like the wheat in her hand.

Libra depicts the moment when Osiris has returned to his place in the world of the dead and continues sitting in judgment over the deceased's actions on Earth. The scales that feature in early Christian iconography is presided over by Thoth, who attends to the exactitude of the measure, assisted by Anubis, who introduces the possible fisherman-to-be. The deceased's earthly deeds are contained in his heart, placed on one of the two trays. On the other tray sits the feather of Maat, exactitude, truth, and cosmic equilibrium. It is hoped the deceased is not "heavy of heart": the two trays should balance perfectly, quite a feat considering the lightness of the feather!

Scorpio: in illustrations decorating the walls of some Late Period temples, the mystery of the miraculous birth of the son of Isis is evoked. The goddess has been fertilized by Osiris after his death, using the magical practices with which we are familiar, but she is alone in her pregnancy to protect her fetus.

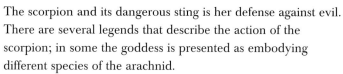

The scorpion and its dangerous sting is her defense against evil. There are several legends that describe the action of the scorpion; in some the goddess is presented as embodying different species of the arachnid.

Sagittarius is presented in the image of a triumphant king pursuing a savage beast with his bow and arrows. Toward the end of the Late Period, he appears as a winged centaur, bow in hand ready to launch its darts. The image is comparable to that of a ruler pursuing evil.

Capricorn: a hybrid animal composed of the forequarters of a goat antelope, often with a fishtail as hindquarters. The creature represents the goat antelope gestating in its mother's womb, half emerged from the water, the seed emerging from the ground.

THE ZODIAC OF VÉZELAY

The order in which the signs of the zodiac are distributed clearly shows where the Egyptians placed their New Year, with the arrival of the flood between Cancer, the scarab, and Leo, the heatwave. However, the start and end of the cycle, Aquarius and Capricorn were placed in the coldest area, at the goddess's feet.

The image of this calendar reproduced on papyrus, as I have described, must have been taken across the Mediterranean by pilgrims and circulated around Europe. It must have appeared many a time on the Lérins Islands where, among the Coptic monks, the future Saint Patrick of Ireland lived.

These manuscripts also no doubt appeared in the library of the abbey of Cluny in France, before reaching other centers of learning. A copy must have also reached architects designing and decorating the church of La Madeleine in Vézelay, central France.

After this review of the zodiac, I invite readers to visit this magnificent and moving monument, especially its narthex. Look up and you will see the fascinating representation of Christ in all his majesty, surrounded by a circular frame containing, in its final half, the motifs of the Egyptian zodiac, miraculously following the same order as they appear in Egypt.

Thus in the far left, the first sign, Aquarius, corresponds to the furthest sign on the right, Capricorn. In order we see: 1.

The zodiac of Vézelay
At the top of the zodiac, aligned with the head of Christ and carved in high relief, are mysterious signs not part of the classical zodiac.
Basilica of La Madeleine, Twelfth century, Vézelay, France

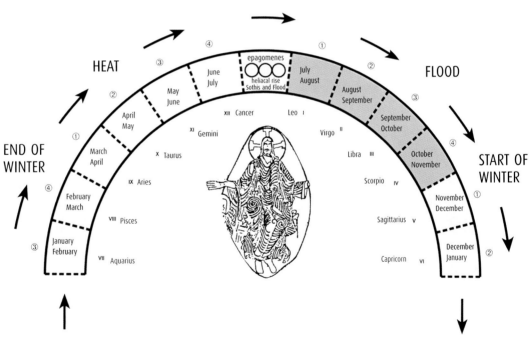

HEAT

FLOOD

END OF
WINTER

START OF
WINTER

epagomenes
heliacal rise
Sothis and Flood

June
July

July
August

May
June

August
September

April
May

September
October

March
April

October
November

February
March

November
December

January
February

December
January

XII Cancer Leo I

XI Gemini Virgo II

X Taurus Libra III

IX Aries Scorpio IV

VIII Pisces Sagittarius V

VII Aquarius Capricorn VI

TOP:

**The basilica of
La Madeleine**

The façade is decorated
with a beautiful collection
of signs of the zodiac.
Basilica of La Madeleine,
Twelfth century,
Vézelay, France

ABOVE:

The zodiac of Vézelay

Each sign of the zodiac, set in a
circle, is accompanied by the
agrarian symbol to which it
corresponds, also set in a similar
circular frame.

Harpocrates
Statuette representing the royal child, Harpocrates, being reborn from the lotus.
Bronze, Saite Period,
Musée du Louvre, Paris

The destiny of Osiris in chrysalis form
The ceilings of several burial chambers in the Valley of the Kings feature representations of the "final hour of night." The spirit of the primal abyss is seen bearing the bark with its scarab passenger, who is pushing the orb of the reborn sun. The chrysalis of Osiris, at the top, will join the solar orb by the action of Isis (the small figure between the sun and the crouching figure of Osiris).
Tomb of Ramses VI,
Twentieth dynasty,
Western Thebes

Aquarius, 2. Pisces, 3. Aries, 4. Taurus, 5. Gemini, 6. Cancer, 7. Leo, 8. Virgo, 9. Libra, 10. Scorpio, 11. Sagittarius, 12. Capricorn. Furthermore, each sign presented in a circle is accompanied by the European agrarian symbol of the month in question. But there is another most unexpected, and extraordinary feature: at the center of this outer half-circle, there are three extra signs situated in line with and above the head of Christ. The signs look Egyptian but do not appear in the Egyptian zodiac and are here inserted between Cancer and Leo without symbolic agrarian explanations.

The first of these signs represents a dog, its legs folded beneath it; next is a mummified body folded up on itself; and finally there is a figure that is half-woman, half-fish. Medievalists have attempted to explain these symbols for hundreds of years, but no explanation so far has proved satisfactory, least of all the suggestion that the middle figure is an acrobat celebrating the feast day of Saint Madeleine at the end of July!

I had a chance, several years ago, to interpret these then opaque images, which seemed potentially comprehensible to an Egyptologist. The first is, of course, the dog Sothis announcing the New Year. The next is the mummy of renascent Osiris, as the hieroglyphic inscription indicates. This figure of Osiris curled in a strange chrysalis position, feet touching his head, as he appears in the final hour of night, can be seen on the ceilings of certain tombs in the Valley of the Kings. Between the head of Osiris and the sun shunted by the scarab is the image of Isis, ensuring the juncture between the two stages, holding up her hands to the reborn star. It is worth noting that this mermaid is one of the oldest known versions of the figure of the siren, announcing the arrival of the inundation.

These three images are extremely resonant, particularly in their ancient Egyptian New Year context: the appearance of the dog Sothis, or rather its reappearance, then Osiris emerging from the chrysalis and greeting the new sun, and finally the arrival of the flood bringing the Distant Goddess, the flood, symbolized by the siren. The three signs sit directly above the image of the Christ in majesty, bringing together the reappearance of the annual cycle and the action of the Creator. The three figures are not actual hieroglyphics and do not feature in Egyptian calendars, but are of Egyptian inspiration dating back to the Christian era. The images, therefore, are genuine puzzles for us and beg many questions: Who designed them? Who assembled them? Who was it who could penetrate Egyptian thinking so incisively that they decorated the narthex of Vézelay basilica with concrete proof of the union between ancient Egyptian scholars and their medieval counterparts? In the Late Period, these signs would have provided faithful illustrations of the twelve months of the Pharaonic calendar without the need for extra commentary. But so far removed from the scholars and scribes of bygone ages, who would have been able to add these three unexpected and highly symbolic images to the later cycle of the signs of the zodiac? Was it a pilgrim monk from the monasteries of Saint Pachomius? Or was it the architects themselves who built the church of La Madeleine?

Whatever the answer to this riddle, the image remains an extraordinary example of this fabulous heritage. And whatever the answer, the figures show that the wonderful heritage of Egypt still has much to teach us about Christ's message, a message to which Egypt was no stranger, long after Pharaonic times. Early Christianity might not have been cut from a Judeo-Christian fabric, as it often said, nor a pagan-Christian weave, as Saint Paul tried to preach. Far from being the fruit of unlikely chance, it is possible it grew from an Egyptian-Christian encounter.

Zodiac of the cathedral of Autun
The three mysterious signs above the head of Christ in the basilica of La Madeleine divide the signs of the zodiac into two equal groups. At the cathedral of Autun in France, the Vézelay trilogy is replaced by a single sign: the squat figure of Harpocrates, the sun-child, legs spread, symbolizing the renewal of the sun, the arrival of the flood, and the New Year.
Twelfth–fifteenth centuries, Saint-Lazare Cathedral, Autun, France

Christ the cosmocrator
This image of Christ surrounded by the twelve signs of the zodiac is from a tenth century manuscript.
Tenth century manuscript, Bibliothèque Nationale, Paris

Notes

CHAPTER XI
The Legacy of Egypt in Israel,
or Joseph and Egypt

1 The total of sixty-six people can be explained by the fact neither Er and Onan, Jacob's sons who died in Canaan, nor Manasse and Ephraim, Joseph's Egyptian-born sons, are included in this figure. The ancient Greek version (v. 27) gives a total of seventy-five, including Joseph's two sons and their five descendants. This figure of seventy is given in Exodus 1:5

2 In a later version, it is said that Joseph calls the region the "Land of Ramses."

3 This paragraph was added later when two older texts, the Elohist and the Yahvist, were brought together. It is extracted from the "sacerdotal code," and it is in this text that we find the region in which Jacob and his family are living is called the "Land of Rameses," located a little further to the north of the land of Goshen.

CHAPTER XII
Wisdom

4 The Hebrews did not have geese. In their transposition of the Egyptian text, the goose is replaced by an eagle.

CHAPTER XIV
The Secret of the Sanctuaries

5 See Otto R. A. Meinardus, *In the Steps of the Holy Family, from Bethlehem to Upper Egypt.* American University in Cairo, 1992.

6 See Gertrud Schiller, *Kunst* vol. 1. Gutersloh, Germany: Verlaghans Gerd Mohn, 1981.

Chronology

PROTOHISTORY

Naqada Period ca. 4000–3100
Narmer

THINITE PERIOD

First dynasty (snake king) ca. 3100–2900
Second dynasty ca. 2900–2700

OLD KINGDOM

Third dynasty (Djoser) ca. 2700–2620
Fourth dynasty (Sneferu, Khufu, Khafra,
    Menkaura, etc.) ca. 2620–2500
Fifth dynasty (Sahura, Nyuserra, etc.)
    ca. 2500–2350
Sixth dynasty (Pepy, etc.) ca. 2350–2200

FIRST INTERMEDIATE PERIOD

Seventh dynasty–start of the 11th dynasty
    ca. 2200–2060

MIDDLE KINGDOM

Eleventh dynasty ca. 2060–2010
Twelfth dynasty (Senusret, Amenemhat, etc.)
    ca. 2010–1786

SECOND INTERMEDIATE PERIOD

Thirteenth–Seventeenth dynasties
    ca. 1786–1555

NEW KINGDOM

Eighteenth dynasty (Amenhotep, Thutmose,
    Hatshepsut, Akhenaten, Tutankhamun, Ay,
    Horemheb) ca. 1555–1305
Nineteenth dynasty (Ramses, Sety, etc.)
    ca. 1305–1196
Twentieth dynasty (Ramses III to XI, etc.)
    ca. 1196–1080

THIRD INTERMEDIATE PERIOD

Twenty-first dynasty (Herihor, etc.)
    ca. 1080–946
Twenty-second dynasty (Osorkon, etc.)
    ca. 946–720
Twenty-third–twenty-fourth dynasties
    ca. 792–712
Twenty-fifth dynasty (Taharqo, Shabaqo, etc.)
    ca. 745–655

LATE PERIOD

Twenty-sixth dynasty (Psamtek II, etc.)
    ca. 664–525
Twenty-seventh–thirtieth dynasties
    ca. 525–342
Second Persian Period ca. 342–332

Ptolemaic Period 332–30 B.C.

Roman Period 30 B.C.–A.D. 337

Coptic Period 337–641

Arabic Period from 641

Further Reading

Allen, James P. *The Art of Medicine in Ancient Egypt.* New York: Metropolitan Museum of Art, 2005.

Andreau, Guillemette, Marie-Hélène Rutschowscaya, and Christiane Ziegler. *Ancient Egypt at the Louvre.* London and New York: I. B. Tauris & Company, 1999.

Arnold, David. *Temples of the Last Pharaohs.* Oxford University Press, 1999.

Catalogue of a Collection of Egyptian Antiquities. Scholarly Publishing Office, University of Michigan Library, 2005.

David, Rosalie. *The Handbook of Life in Ancient Egypt.* Oxford University Press, 1999.

Desroches-Noblecourt, Christiane. *Great Pharaoh Ramses and His Time.* New York: Hacker Art Books, 1988.

Desroches-Noblecourt, Christiane. *The World Saves Abu Simbel.* Berlin: Verlaf AF Koska, 1968.

Desroches-Noblecourt, Christiane. *Tutankhamun: Life and Death of a Pharaoh.* London: Book Club Associates, 1971.

Dodson, Aidan and Dyan Hilton. *The Complete Royal Families of Ancient Egypt: A Genealogical Sourcebook of the Pharaohs.* London: Thames & Hudson, 2004.

Hare, Tom. *Remembering Osiris: Number, Gender, and the Word in Ancient Egyptian Representational Systems.* Palo Alto, CA: Stanford University Press, 1999.

Hawass, Zahi. *Hidden Treasures of Ancient Egypt: Unearthing the Masterpieces of the Egyptian Museum in Cairo.* Washington, D.C.: National Geographic, 2004.

Hawass, Zahi. *Tutankhamun and the Golden Age of the Pharaohs: Official Companion Book to the Exhibition Sponsored by National Geographic.* Washington, D.C.: National Geographic, 2005.

James, T. G. H. *Pharaoh's People: Scenes From Life in Imperial Egypt.* University of Chicago Press, 1986.

James, T. G. H. *Ramses II.* New York: Friedman/Fairfax, 2002.

Redford, Donald, B. *The Ancient Gods Speak: A Guide to Egyptian Religion.* Oxford University Press, 2002.

Reeves, C. N., Richard H. Wilkinson, and Nicholas Reeves. *The Complete Valley of the Kings: Tombs and Treasures of Egypt's Greatest Pharaohs.* London: Thames & Hudson, 1996.

Reeves, Nicholas. *The Complete Tutankhumun: The King, the Tomb, the Royal Treasure.* London: Thames & Hudson, 1995.

Roehrig, Catharine H., Renee Dreyfus, and Cathleen A. Keller, eds. *Hatshepsut: From Queen to Pharaoh.* New York: Metropolitan Museum of Art, 2005.

Rosellini, Ippolito. *The Monuments of Egypt and Nubia.* American University in Cairo Press, 2003.

Smith, G. Elliot. *The Ancient Egyptians and Their Influence upon the Civilization of Europe 1911.* Kila, MT: Kessinger Publishing, 2004.

Strudwick, Nigel and Helen Strudwick. *Thebes in Egypt: A Guide to the Tombs and Temples of Ancient Egypt.* Ithaca, N.Y.: Cornell University Press, 1999.

Tyldesley, Joyce A. *Daughters of Isis: Women of Ancient Egypt.* London: Penguin Books, 1995.

Velikovsky, Immanuel. *Ramses II and His Time.* Book World Promotions, 1978.

Verner, Miroslav. *The Pyramids: The Mystery, Culture, and Science of Egypt's Great Monuments.* Berkeley, CA: Grove Press, 2002.